RAND McNALLY READING PROGRAM
Young America Basic Series

RAND McNALLY READING PROGRAM
Young America Basic Series

Leo Fay
Professor of Education, Indiana University

Ramon Royal Ross
Professor of Education, San Diego State University

Margaret LaPray
Professor of Education, San Diego State University

Rand McNally & Company / Chicago

Moonbeams
and
Microscopes

Contents

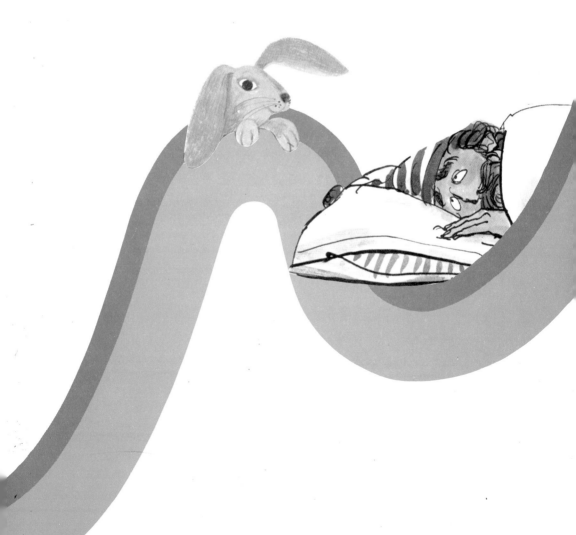

Snips
and
Snails

8

Rules

Karla Kuskin

Do not jump on ancient uncles,

Do not yell at average mice,

Do not wear a broom to breakfast,

Do not ask a snake's advice.

Do not bathe in chocolate pudding,

Do not talk to bearded bears.

Do not smoke cigars on sofas,

Do not dance on velvet chairs.

Do not take a whale to visit

Russell's mother's cousin's yacht.

And whatever else you do

It is better you

Do not.

From Alexander Soames: His Poems by Karla Kuskin. Copyright © 1962 by Karla Kuskin. Reprinted by permission of Harper & Row, Publishers.

One Thing After Another

"Teddy," Mrs. Davis called, "we're out of eggs. Your father must have eaten the last ones for breakfast."

Teddy pretended not to hear his mother. He usually enjoyed going to the store, but right now he was working with a piece of wood. Teddy liked to work with wood, and his parents had just given him a new wood-burning set.

"Will you get some eggs at the store, Teddy?" Mrs. Davis asked. "I can't bake a cake without eggs."

"Couldn't we have cake tomorrow?" asked Teddy.

Mrs. Davis stared at Teddy and said, "Theodore!" When Mrs. Davis called him Theodore in that tone of voice, Teddy knew that his mother meant business. So he went to get his bike.

Teddy waved to his mother as he rode his bike down the walk. When he got past the front of the house, the lady next door called to him.

"Oh, Teddy," Mrs. Moon cried. "Are you going to the store?"

Teddy looked at her. He knew what was coming. Mrs. Moon liked to have Teddy do errands for her. She never asked Teddy if he liked doing errands for her.

"I just need some carrots," Mrs. Moon told him. "I'm sure you can get me some carrots."

"No, ma'am. I mean, yes, ma'am," Teddy said. "Oh, well," he thought, "I guess it wouldn't take that much longer to get the carrots, too."

Teddy rode on down the street. At the third house Mr. Peters was raking leaves.

"Say, Teddy," Mr. Peters said. "Are you going to the store?"

"Yes, sir," Teddy answered. "But I have to hurry. Mom needs eggs right away."

"Oh, this won't take you more than a minute," Mr. Peters said. "I'm out of dog food. You know the kind I always get."

"Yes, sir," Teddy said. He got back on his bike. Dog food for Mr. Peters, carrots for Mrs. Moon, and eggs for his mom—that wouldn't take too long.

Across the street Mrs. Valentine was walking her dog. "Why, Theodore," she called, "how nice to see you."

Mrs. Valentine was one of Teddy's favorite people. She traveled so much on business for her company that Teddy didn't get to see her very often. But when he did, she was always cheerful.

"Are you going to the store?" she asked.

"Yes," Teddy answered.

"I'm really sorry to bother you," she said, "but my plane leaves in an hour, and I just lost a button. Could you please get some white thread for me?"

Teddy just couldn't refuse. As he pedaled away, he shook his head—white thread for Mrs. Valentine, dog food for Mr. Peters, carrots for Mrs. Moon, and eggs for his mom.

"It's too bad it's not raining," Teddy thought. "If it were, everyone would be inside, and they wouldn't be thinking of things for me to do."

Just then a voice called, "Yoo-hoo! Young man!" Teddy tried to pretend that he didn't hear. But Mrs. Pool had a voice so loud that it made the walls shake. She knew Teddy's name, but she always called him "young man."

"Where are you going, young man?" Mrs. Pool shouted. She always wanted to know where he was going. She liked to know everything that went on.

"I'm going to the store. Mom needs eggs in a hurry," Teddy explained.

"Is your mother baking?" Mrs. Pool asked loudly. Teddy nodded. By now everyone on the street knew that his mom was baking today.

"That's a good idea," she said. "I think I'll bake, too. I'll make cookies. Be a good boy, young man, and get me some flour. Can you remember to do that?"

Teddy shook his head and started off. Flour for Mrs. Pool, white thread for Mrs. Valentine, dog food for Mr. Peters, carrots for Mrs. Moon, and eggs for his mom. Flour for Mrs. Pool, white thread . . . .

Teddy took all the back streets to the store. He didn't want anyone else to know where he was going.

Teddy parked his bike near the door and ran into the store. He took one of the carts, raced to the vegetable counter, and got the carrots. Then he raced down the next aisle where he found the flour. He was in such a hurry that he nearly ran into a couple of people. But Teddy didn't want to take all day running errands! Why have a new wood-burning set if he didn't have enough time to use it?

Teddy stopped to think what was next. He remembered! After Teddy got the white thread, he had no trouble finding the dog food.

Ah, that was everything! Suddenly Teddy couldn't remember if he forgot anything. He stood still and thought: carrots for Mrs. Moon, dog food for Mr. Peters, white thread for Mrs. Valentine, and flour for Mrs. Pool. Teddy checked in the cart and everything was there.

Each thing was wrapped in a different bag, and soon Teddy was on his way. His first stop was going to be Mrs. Pool's house.

"Here's your flour," Teddy said, handing her a heavy package.

"Right, young man," Mrs. Pool shouted. "You come over tonight, and I'll give you some cookies."

Teddy thanked her and went to find Mrs. Valentine.

"Here's your white thread," Teddy said when he found her.

"Thank you, Theodore," she said. "Thank you very much."

Mr. Peters was still raking leaves when Teddy gave him the dog food.

"I like a boy who doesn't forget things," Mr. Peters told him. "Thank you, Teddy."

Teddy didn't have to look for Mrs. Moon, because she was waiting for him.

"Have you got my carrots?" she asked. "These are nice carrots," she said. "You're a good little shopper, Teddy."

Teddy sighed. At last, he was finished. Now he could get back to his wood burning. Teddy stopped suddenly. "The eggs!" he cried. "I forgot the eggs!"

He started to go back to the store, but his mother opened the door.

"Well, Teddy!" she said. "Did you go to the moon and back?"

Teddy closed his eyes. "I forgot the eggs," he said very softly. "But I'll go right back and . . ."

He stopped talking when he saw his mother laughing.

"Poor Teddy!" she said. "It's been one thing after another for you, hasn't it?"

"How did you know?" Teddy was puzzled.

"You were gone so long that I telephoned the store. They told me about all the shopping you did for the neighbors and also that there weren't any eggs in the shopping cart. So I guessed you forgot," she smiled.

"I'll go right back and get them for you," said Teddy.

"That's okay," she said. "I asked the man to send someone over with them. I guess I could have done that in the first place."

Teddy went back to his wood-burning set. "Grown-ups!" he thought. "They always think of the easy way when it's too late."

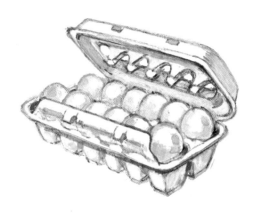

Grupatupsky

Grupatupsky was a wonderful magician. "The King of Magicians" he was called. He wore a black top hat and a black silk cape. Over his shoulder he carried a big red velvet bag.

In Grupatupsky's bag was all his magic. No one but Grupatupsky had ever looked in that bag. And he never told anyone about the magic in it. When people asked him how he did his tricks, he would just smile and say, "That I never will tell."

Grupatupsky traveled from town to town. In every town he gave a magic show. And what magic shows he gave!

Out of his red velvet bag he pulled dogs, birds, and rosebushes. He turned his black hat red, then blue, then black again.

People cheered and clapped their hands. "How do you do it, Grupatupsky?" they cried. "How do you do it?"

But he always answered, "That I never will tell."

Other magicians tried to find out the secrets of Grupatupsky's magic. Magicians hid behind the stage while he did his magic show. They hid in his hotel room—behind the curtains, under the bed, and in the bathtub. They all hoped to peek into the red velvet bag.

But Grupatupsky always found them, and he never let his red velvet bag out of his sight.

One day Grupatupsky got off a train at Piper Pass. It was the first time he had ever been there. He had planned a very special show. His red velvet bag bulged with magic.

That night the school auditorium was filled. All the people of Piper Pass were there because everyone wanted to see Grupatupsky, the King of Magicians.

At last Grupatupsky came out onto the stage. The audience grew very quiet. The magician gave a low, deep bow, and as he bowed, he removed his top hat. Out of the hat flew six snow-white doves. Around and around they flew, over the heads of the audience. And then they flew back to sit on Grupatupsky's shoulders. Grupatupsky bowed again.

The audience clapped and whistled and cheered—all but one little boy. Of course, Grupatupsky noticed him right away. The boy sat quietly in his seat. He didn't laugh. He didn't clap. He didn't even smile. He just looked at Grupatupsky.

Grupatupsky gave the best show he had ever given. Twelve little rabbits jumped out of his hat. They did somersaults around the stage. Then they jumped back into the hat.

But the quiet little boy sat still in his seat. All the other children called out, "How did you do that, Grupatupsky?" All of them laughed and clapped. And still the quiet little boy just looked and looked.

Grupatupsky decided he just had to make that little boy laugh. He swirled his cape. Out came six dancing dogs. He pulled a rosebush out of his big red bag. It grew before everybody's eyes until it became a rose tree. He threw a rope up into the air. It stood up all by itself.

Grupatupsky pulled trick after trick out of his bag. People gasped, "Oh!" and "Ah!" They cried, "How do you do it?"

Grupatupsky's deep voice boomed, "That I never will tell!"

But the quiet little boy never cheered or laughed. He just looked.

27

At last the show came to an end, and Grupatupsky did his last trick. He bowed to the people who cheered wildly for him. But he was not happy. He never made that little boy laugh, and he didn't know why.

In fact, the little boy was no longer in his seat. "I guess he left early," Grupatupsky thought. "I guess he didn't like the show at all."

He picked up his big red velvet bag. It was heavier than usual. "How strange," thought the King of Magicians.

He walked to his hotel room. He closed the door. He looked under the bed. He looked in the bathtub. He looked behind the curtains. No magicians were there.

Then he opened his red velvet bag. Out came his dogs. Out came his doves. Out came his rabbits. And out came a surprise! Grupatupsky rubbed his eyes and looked again, for there was the quiet little boy climbing out of the red velvet bag.

"Oh!" gasped Grupatupsky. "My boy!" he cried. "How ever did you get in my bag? Tell me quickly! How did you do it?"

The little boy looked at Grupatupsky. "That I never will tell," he said. And then, at last, the little boy laughed.

Every Time I Climb a Tree

David McCord

Every time I climb a tree
Every time I climb a tree
Every time I climb a tree
I scrape a leg
Or skin a knee
And every time I climb a tree
I find some ants
Or dodge a bee
And get the ants
All over me

From Far and Few *by David McCord, by permission of Little, Brown and Co. Copyright © 1952 by David McCord.*

And every time I climb a tree
Where have you been?
They say to me
But don't they know that I am free
Every time I climb a tree?
I like it best
To spot a nest
That has an egg
Or maybe three

And then I skin
The other leg
But every time I climb a tree
I see a lot of things to see
Swallows rooftops and TV
And all the fields and farms there be
Every time I climb a tree
Though climbing may be good for ants
It isn't awfully good for pants
But still it's pretty good for me
Every time I climb a tree

⌐ A Special Place

Many people have special things they do or special places where they go when they want to feel better. In the poem you just read, climbing a tree was special to the boy.

Do you have a different place or a different thing you like to do?

If something is special to you, you might not want to tell *all* about it. But you can tell a little about it by writing a riddle or a poem or by drawing a picture. Choose a way to tell others about something special to you.

33

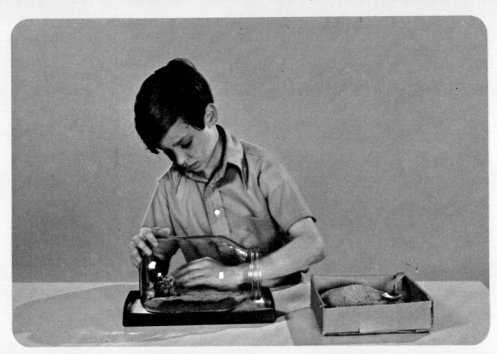

How to Make a Terrarium

How would you like to have a desert or a woodland growing in your classroom?

Does this sound like something only a magician could do? Well, it isn't. It is something that you can do at school. With just a few things you can make yourself a terrarium. A terrarium can hold many wonderful worlds!

You can make a desert terrarium and a woodland terrarium. To begin, you will need these things:

1. two gallon jars with wide mouths
2. two pounds of plaster of Paris
3. two shoe-box lids

Now mix the plaster of Paris with some water. Use just enough water to make a thick mixture. Stir it until it is smooth.

Pour half of the mixture into one shoe-box lid and the other half into the other shoe-box lid.

Set a gallon jar on its side in each box of plaster. Let them set for an hour until the plaster is hard and dry.

And now you are ready to plant your two terrariums.

A Desert Terrarium

A beautiful desert terrarium is easy to make. Here are the things that you need:

1. some soil
2. some sand
3. a few rocks
4. some tiny cactus plants

First put the soil into the bottom of your terrarium. Then cover the soil with sand.

Plant the cactus plants here and there in the sand.

Then scatter the rocks in the terrarium. These make it look like a real desert.

Water your plants lightly once a week. Don't use very much water. Too much water will kill cactus plants.

A Woodland Terrarium

Another beautiful terrarium that you can make is a woodland terrarium. You will need:

1. some charcoal
2. some gravel
3. some soil
4. a jar lid
5. ferns and mosses
6. a few tiny green garden plants

First mix the charcoal, gravel, and soil together. Put the mixture into the bottom of your terrarium.

Now put the jar lid in the soil and plant your ferns, mosses, and other plants in the soil around the lid. Fill the lid with water so that it looks like a small lake.

Add a little water to the soil. Then put a
lid on your terrarium. If you keep the lid on
your terrarium, you won't have to add
water to the soil for a long time.

A Different Day

This was Pete's first day in a new school. Throughout the entire day, none of the other students spoke to him. They were waiting, curious to see how Jeff would treat him.

Although the other boys played games with Jeff, they didn't really like him. They were afraid of him because he was big and a bully.

After school, Jeff and some other kids waited for Pete in the alley. Everyone knew Jeff would dare the new boy to fight. Everyone knew the fight would be unfair, because Jeff was bigger than Pete.

But everyone continued to wait, anxious to see whether Pete would run or be foolish enough to fight Jeff.

When Pete came out, Jeff quickly approached him. He stepped right in front of Pete.

"Hey, kid!" Jeff called. "You're new around here." He wanted to show Pete that he didn't like new boys.

"Yes," said Pete. He didn't run. He just looked at Jeff. Then he looked at the others. He knew why they were all waiting for him. Pete had seen boys like Jeff in other schools.

Jeff picked up a rock and put it on his hand. He held his hand out to show Pete the rock. He said, "Take the rock off my hand. Go on. I dare you!"

"We dare you, too!" some boys called.

Pete asked, "Is this a new game?"

Jeff said, "Go on! I dare you! Take the rock off my hand. Go on! You'll find out what this game is."

Pete took the rock off Jeff's hand. "Now you have to fight!" Jeff said.

"Fight! Fight!" the boys shouted. They
didn't care that Pete was not as big as Jeff.

Pete didn't like this game. "Why do we
have to fight?" he asked.

Jeff laughed. "I knew it! I knew you were
afraid of me!" he shouted. And he gave
Pete a big push.

Pete didn't like to be pushed. He said,
"Don't do that! Don't push me!"

"I'll push you if I want," Jeff bragged. "I'll do anything I want, because I'm in charge here! Unless you're tough enough to stop me."

"Pete's a coward," the boys shouted. "Dare him to fight!"

"No, I'm not a coward," said Pete calmly.

"Then fight!" demanded Jeff.

"I'll fight, but tell me why we're fighting," Pete said.

"I whip all new kids," Jeff chuckled.

"Why?" Pete asked.

"So they're absolutely sure who the boss is here," Jeff said impatiently.

"You're not a boss, just a bully," declared Pete. "Why do you toss your weight around?"

"I like it that way," Jeff said, flashing a nasty smile.

Pete looked at the other boys. "Do they like it that way?" he asked.

Jeff laughed. He knew they didn't like it, but they were afraid of him. "Who cares what they like! I'll show you I'm boss. John," he shouted," come over here!"

A little boy came running to Jeff. But he didn't look happy about it.

"Give me your coat," ordered Jeff.

John didn't want to give Jeff his coat. But he didn't dare fight. So he handed his coat to the bigger boy.

Jeff took it and flung it down. Then he jumped up and down on John's coat. It got dirty, but Jeff didn't care.

"Why did you do that to his coat?" Pete asked. "You're bigger than he is. You're bigger than all the boys. They can't fight back. Do you like to have other boys afraid of you?"

"Sure," said Jeff.

"Well," said Pete, "I'm not afraid."

Again, Jeff gave Pete a push. "Sure you are," he said. "Sure you are."

But he could see Pete didn't show he was
afraid. Jeff didn't know why. After all,
Pete was just a little boy, and Jeff was a
bigger boy.

Jeff didn't like it. He wanted this new
boy to be afraid. "Come on, new boy!" Jeff
shouted. "Are you ready?"

"Yes," Pete said. "Are *you* ready?"

Jeff laughed. "I could whip you with one
hand in back of me!" he said.

Then John came over and picked up his
coat. "I'll help Pete," he said.

"I'll make you sorry for that, runt," Jeff growled. "But first keep out of the way for a moment, while I take care of this new kid."

"No," said John quietly. "No, I'm going to help Pete." John felt afraid, but still he did not step back from the bully.

Pete said, "No, I don't need help."

Jeff and Pete put up their fists, ready to fight. Just as Jeff started to throw the first punch, something happened. Somehow, Pete quickly grabbed Jeff's hand and by pulling it, flung the bigger boy's entire body to the ground.

Jeff got up, but Pete was ready for him. Jeff shoved Pete. Again Pete threw him. The bully's legs wobbled, and he was not sure he could get up.

"What happened? How did you do that?" a surprised Jeff asked. "You threw me!"

"My dad showed me how to fight a bigger kid and win," Pete said. "He taught me to move quickly before a bigger kid is ready."

John looked unhappy. "Are you the boss, Pete? Do I have to fight you now?"

"Oh no," said Pete. "My dad also told me to fight only when necessary. Let's play."

Now the other boys came up to Pete.
They, too, did not look happy.

"You threw Jeff. Do we all have to fight
you now?" one boy asked.

"No," Pete said. "There will be no more fighting. There will be no more shoving around. Why don't we have fun? I just want to be friends."

The boys were ready to play games. They all ran back to the school yard.

Pete shouted, "Come on, John! Don't you want to play, too?"

John said, "Sure! It's good to have a friend like you!"

Before Breakfast

"Where's Papa going with that ax?" said Fern to her mother as they were setting the table for breakfast.

"Out to the hoghouse," replied Mrs. Arable. "Some pigs were born last night."

"I don't see why he needs an ax," continued Fern, who was only eight.

"Well," said her mother, "one of the pigs is a runt. It's very small and weak and it will never amount to anything. So your father has decided to do away with it."

"Do *away* with it?" shrieked Fern. "You mean *kill* it? Just because it's smaller than the others?"

Mrs. Arable put a pitcher of cream on the table. "Don't yell, Fern!" she said. "Your father is right. The pig would probably die anyway."

Fern pushed a chair out of the way and ran outdoors. The grass was wet, and the earth smelled of springtime. Fern's sneakers were sopping by the time she caught up with her father.

"Please don't kill it!" she sobbed. "It's unfair."

Mr. Arable stopped walking.

"Fern," he said gently, "you will have to learn to control yourself."

"Control myself?" yelled Fern. "This is a matter of life and death, and you talk about *controlling* myself." Tears ran down her cheeks and she took hold of the ax and tried to pull it out of her father's hand.

"Fern," said Mr. Arable, "I know more about raising a litter of pigs than you do. A weakling makes trouble. Now run along!"

"But it's unfair," cried Fern. "The pig couldn't help being born small, could it? If *I* had been very small at birth, would you have killed *me*?"

Mr. Arable smiled. "Certainly not," he said, looking down at his daughter with love. "But this is different. A little girl is one thing, a little runty pig is another."

"I see no difference," replied Fern, still hanging on to the ax. "This is the most terrible case of injustice I ever heard of."

A queer look came over John Arable's face. He seemed almost ready to cry himself.

"All right," he said. "You go back to the house and I will bring the runt when I come in. I'll let you start it on a bottle, like a baby. Then you'll see what trouble a pig can be."

When Mr. Arable returned to the house half an hour later, he carried a carton under his arm. Fern was upstairs changing her sneakers. The kitchen table was set for breakfast, and the room smelled of coffee, bacon, damp plaster, and wood smoke from the stove.

"Put it on her chair!" said Mrs. Arable. Mr. Arable set the carton down at Fern's place. Then he walked to the sink and washed his hands and dried them on the roller towel.

Fern came slowly down the stairs. Her eyes were red from crying. As she approached her chair, the carton wobbled, and there was a scratching noise. Fern looked at her father. Then she lifted the lid of the carton. There, inside, looking up at her, was the newborn pig. It was a white one. The morning light shone through its ears, turning them pink.

"He's yours," said Mr. Arable. "Saved from an untimely death. And may the good Lord forgive me for this foolishness."

Fern couldn't take her eyes off the tiny pig. "Oh," she whispered. "Oh, *look* at him! He's absolutely perfect."

She closed the carton carefully. First she kissed her father, then she kissed her mother. Then she opened the lid again, lifted the pig out, and held it against her cheek. At this moment her brother Avery came into the room. Avery was ten. He was heavily armed—an air rifle in one hand, a wooden dagger in the other.

"What's that?" he demanded. "What's Fern got?"

"She's got a guest for breakfast," said Mrs. Arable. "Wash your hands and face, Avery!"

"Let's see it!" said Avery, setting his gun down. "You call that miserable thing a pig? That's a *fine* specimen of a pig—it's no bigger than a white rat."

"Wash up and eat your breakfast, Avery!" said his mother. "The school bus will be along in half an hour."

"Can I have a pig, too, Pop?" asked Avery.

"No, I only distribute pigs to early risers," said Mr. Arable. "Fern was up at daylight, trying to rid the world of injustice. As a result, she now has a pig. A small one, to be sure, but nevertheless a pig. It just shows what can happen if a person gets out of bed promptly. Let's eat!"

But Fern couldn't eat until her pig had had a drink of milk. Mrs. Arable found a baby's nursing bottle and a rubber nipple. She poured warm milk into the bottle, fitted the nipple over the top, and handed it to Fern. "Give him his breakfast!" she said.

A minute later, Fern was seated on the floor in the corner of the kitchen with her infant between her knees, teaching it to suck from the bottle. The pig, although tiny, had a good appetite and caught on quickly.

The school bus honked from the road.

"Run!" commanded Mrs. Arable, taking the pig from Fern and slipping a doughnut into her hand. Avery grabbed his gun and another doughnut.

The children ran out to the road and climbed into the bus. Fern took no notice of the others in the bus. She just sat and stared out of the window, thinking what a blissful world it was and how lucky she was to have entire charge of a pig. By the time the bus reached school, Fern had named her pet, selecting the most beautiful name she could think of.

"Its name is Wilbur," she whispered to herself.

She was still thinking about the pig when the teacher said: "Fern, what is the capital of Pennsylvania?"

"Wilbur," replied Fern, dreamily. The pupils giggled. Fern blushed.

More About Wilbur

The story of Fern's pig, Wilbur, doesn't end here. "Before Breakfast" is only the first chapter of a book called *Charlotte's Web,* by E. B. White. In the book, Wilbur grows up into a fine, stout pig who brings great joy to Fern.

Wilbur is befriended by a most unusual spider named Charlotte. Charlotte thinks that Wilbur is really just a little bit silly, especially when he brags that he could make a spider web—and then tries to!

Yet Charlotte loves Wilbur, and when he finds out that he is to be butchered in the fall, it is Charlotte who works out a way to save him.

The adventures of Wilbur, Charlotte, and a very selfish rat named Templeton will make you laugh and maybe even cry a little bit. But most of all, it will make you very happy that you read it.

Through Many Moons

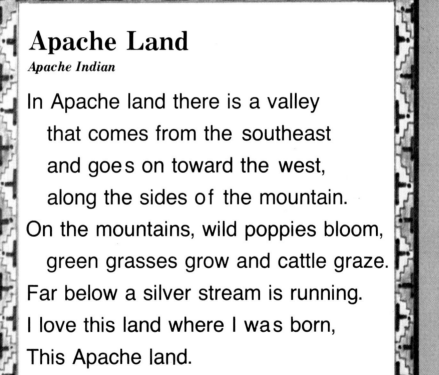

Apache Land
Apache Indian

In Apache land there is a valley
   that comes from the southeast
   and goes on toward the west,
   along the sides of the mountain.
On the mountains, wild poppies bloom,
   green grasses grow and cattle graze.
Far below a silver stream is running.
I love this land where I was born,
This Apache land.

⌐ Facts About Picture Writing

Early people were different from animals because they could talk to other people. They could also draw pictures. For many, many years pictures were the written language of humans. Picture writing, or *pictography,* has been used in all parts of the world.

North American Indians drew pictures of things. But they also drew many pictures of people doing things. The Indians had pictographs for people running, for people shooting, and for other acts.

Indian writing was put on bark, buffalo hides, and stones.

Sometimes the Indians drew pictures for ideas. An arrow might mean *war*. A pipe might stand for *peace*.

The Plains Indians went many, many miles to look for food. They met Indians from many other tribes. They usually did not talk the same language. But they could talk to each other with picture writing.

Once two Indian tribes told each other they would not have any more wars. A pictograph of two clasped hands shows this happening.

Picture writing was important for early people. It is important for us, too. We can read the pictures early humans left behind. Because we have their picture writing, we can find out things about the people who lived before us.

⌐ Painted Pony Runs Away

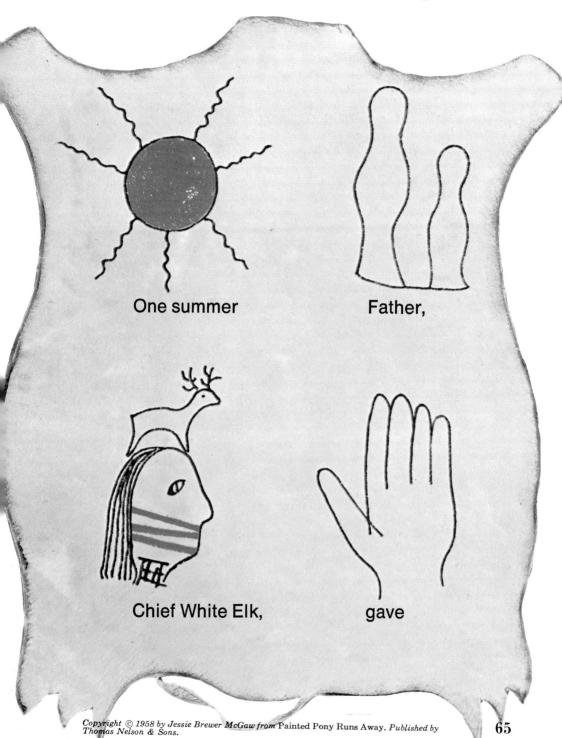

One summer

Father,

Chief White Elk,

gave

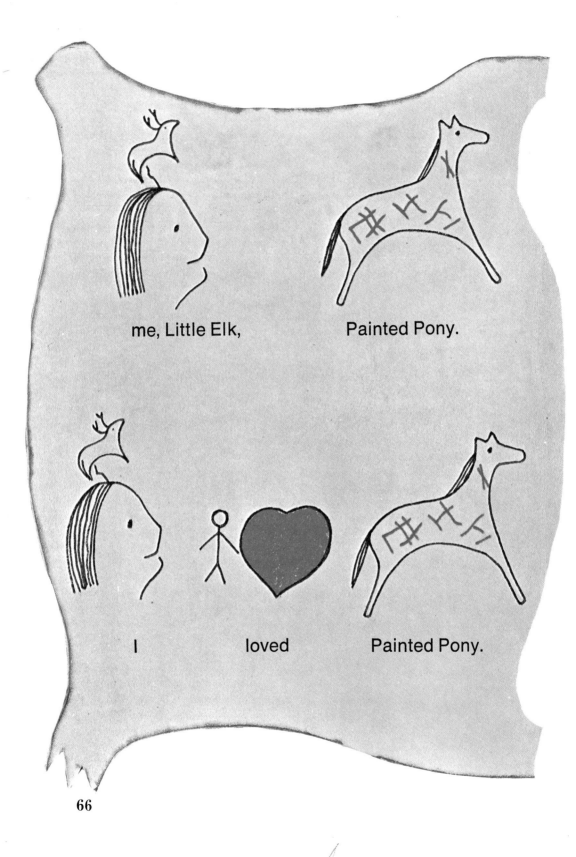

me, Little Elk,   Painted Pony.

I   loved   Painted Pony.

66

I

was happy.

On fourteenth day   of rose moon

I

untied Painted Pony

and left

for ride.

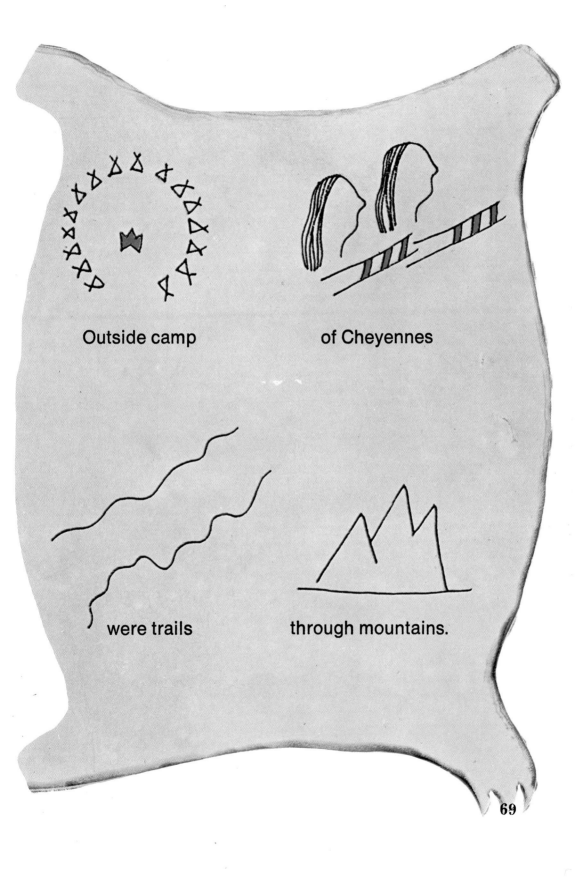

Outside camp

of Cheyennes

were trails

through mountains.

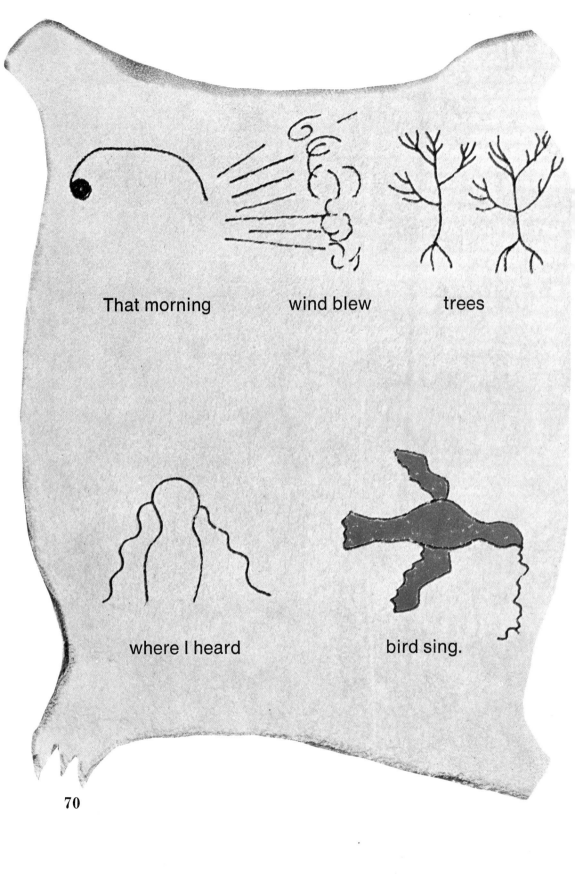

That morning   wind blew   trees

where I heard   bird sing.

Farther on

I saw

porcupine,

antelope,

and moose.

71

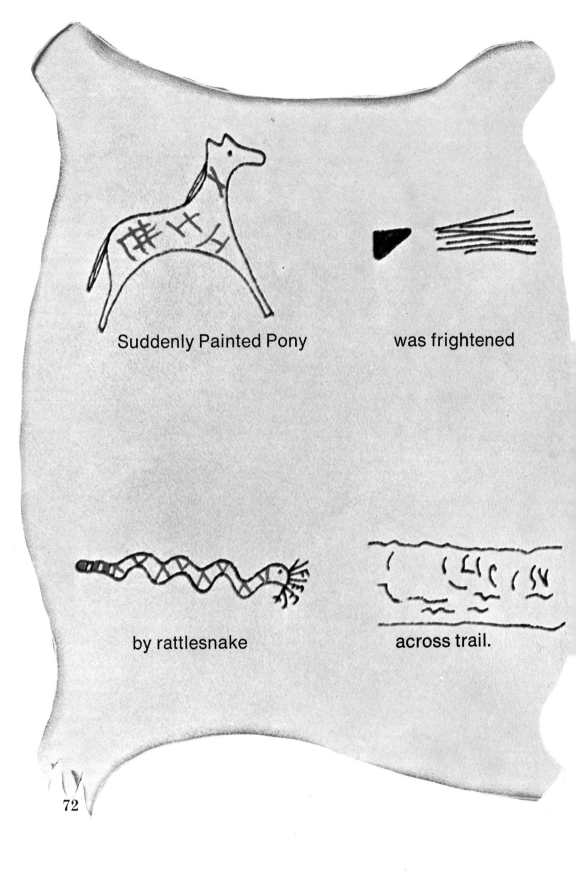

Suddenly Painted Pony

was frightened

by rattlesnake

across trail.

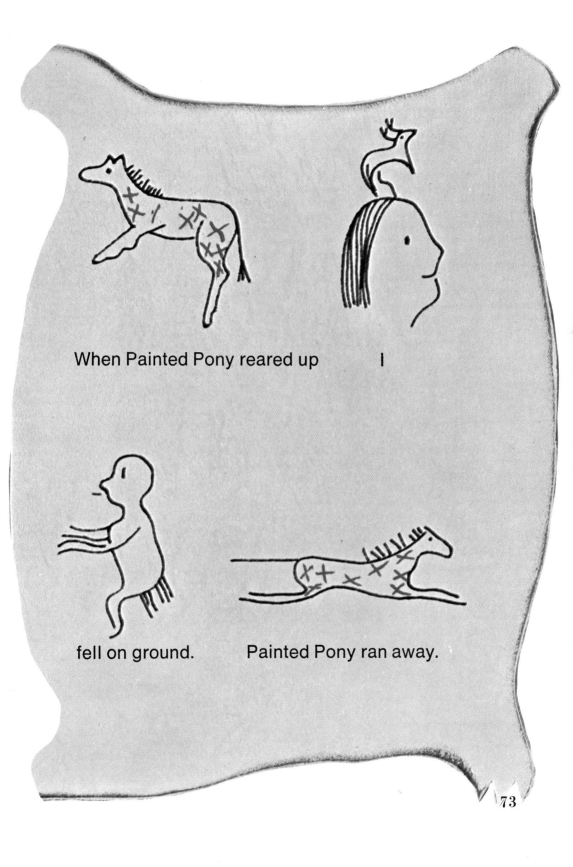

When Painted Pony reared up   I

fell on ground.   Painted Pony ran away.

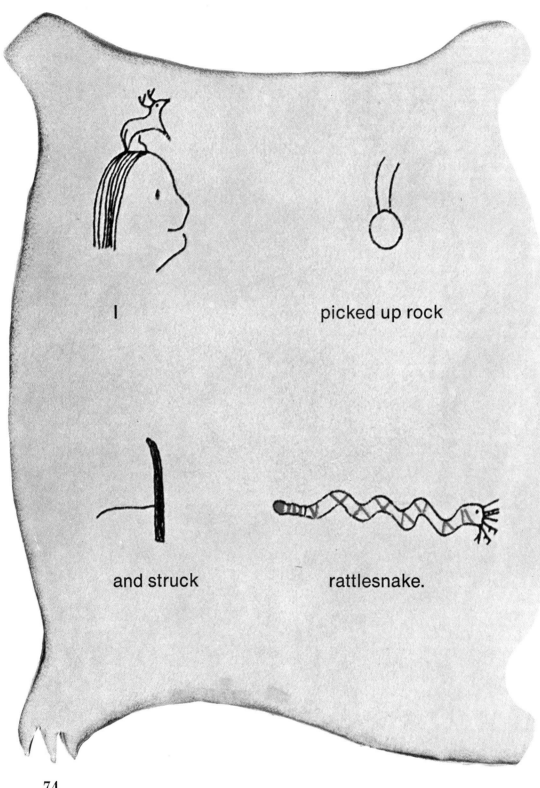

I   picked up rock

and struck   rattlesnake.

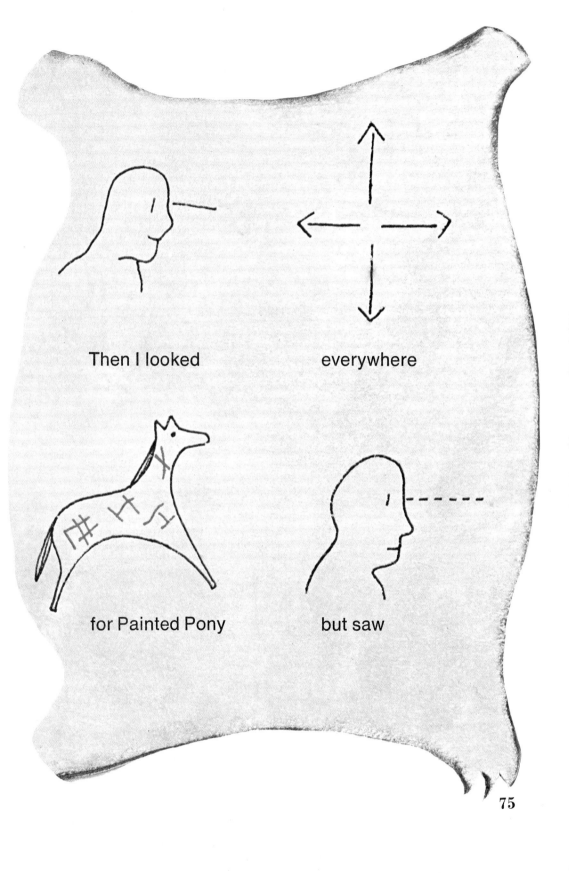

Then I looked   everywhere

for Painted Pony   but saw

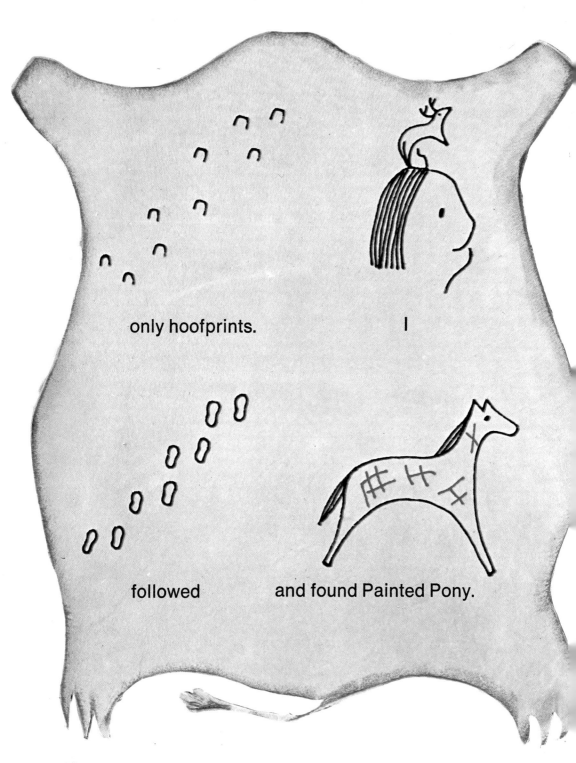

only hoofprints.

I

followed

and found Painted Pony.

The Eagle and the Boy

One day the Indian boy, Waukewa, was hunting along the mountainside. He saw a young eagle with a broken wing. It was lying at the base of a cliff.

The bird had fallen from its nest high above. It was too young to fly and had fluttered down the cliff. Now it was so badly hurt that it was likely to die.

When Waukewa saw the eagle, he was about to drive one of his sharp arrows through its body. He remembered that the eagle often robs many a fine fish from the Indian's drying frame. But when he saw the young bird quivering with pain and fright at his feet, he stopped.

Waukewa slowly unbent his bow. He put the arrow in his quiver and stooped over the frightened eaglet. For fully a minute the wild eyes of the wounded bird and the eyes of the Indian boy looked into one another.

Then the quivering of the young eagle stopped. The wild, frightened look passed out of its eyes. It let Waukewa pass his hand gently over its feathers. From that moment Waukewa and the eagle were friends.

Slowly Waukewa went home to his father's lodge. He carried the wounded eaglet in his arms. He held it so gently that the broken wing gave no pain. The bird lay perfectly still, never even trying to strike the boy's hands.

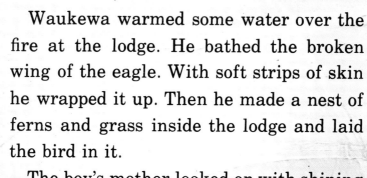

Waukewa warmed some water over the fire at the lodge. He bathed the broken wing of the eagle. With soft strips of skin he wrapped it up. Then he made a nest of ferns and grass inside the lodge and laid the bird in it.

The boy's mother looked on with shining eyes. Her heart was very kind. From her girlhood she had loved all the animals of the woods. It pleased her to see her own gentle ways in the boy.

When Waukewa's father returned from hunting, he saw the wounded bird. He would have caught it up and broken its neck, but Waukewa begged him not to. The boy stood over the bird, guarding it with his small hands. His father laughed and called him his "little squawheart."

"Keep it, then," he said. "Nurse it until it is well. But then you must let it go. We will not raise a thief in the lodges."

So Waukewa promised that when the eagle's wing was healed, he would give it its freedom.

It was one moon before the young eagle's wing had fully healed. Now the bird was old enough and strong enough to fly. The boy had cared for it and fed it daily. The friendship between Waukewa and the bird had grown very strong.

81

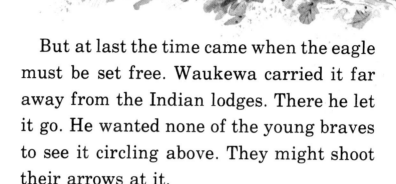

But at last the time came when the eagle must be set free. Waukewa carried it far away from the Indian lodges. There he let it go. He wanted none of the young braves to see it circling above. They might shoot their arrows at it.

The young eagle rose up to the sky in great circles. It was happy with its freedom and its new power of flight.

Then Waukewa began to move away from the spot. But the eagle came rushing down again. All day long it followed him through the woods as he hunted.

At sunset Waukewa started back to the Indian lodges. The eagle would have gone with him, but the boy suddenly slipped into a hollow tree and hid. After a long time the eagle stopped sweeping about in search of the boy. Slowly and sadly, the young bird flew away.

Summer passed, and then winter. Spring came again, with its flowers and birds. Fish filled the lakes and streams. Then it was that all the Indians, old and young, braves and squaws, pushed their canoes out from shore. With the spear and hook they caught the salmon and the large red-spotted trout.

After the long winter it was a joy to work in the sunshine and the warm wind. And the baked fish was good after a winter of dried meats and corn!

Above the great falls of the Apahoqui, the salmon played in the cool, rushing water. They darted under the rocks and leaped out into the cool air. Nowhere else were there such large salmon. Those which swam in the river at the head of the Apahoqui rapids were the biggest of all.

But only the most daring braves went to look for them there, for that part of the river was dangerous. Should a light canoe once pass the danger point, it would get caught in the rush of the rapids. Then nothing could save it from going over the roaring falls.

Now it was very early in the morning of a clear April day. The sun was rising over the mountains. Waukewa put his canoe in the water a half mile above the rapids of the Apahoqui.

He floated downward, spear in hand. Waukewa was the only Indian boy who dared fish above the falls. But he had been there often. Never had his watchful eye and his strong paddle let the river carry his canoe beyond the danger point.

This morning he was alone on the river. He had risen long before daylight to be first at the spot.

The river was full of salmon. They were big, healthy fellows that swam about the canoe on every side in an endless silver stream. Waukewa drove his spear right and left and tossed one shining fish after another into the bark canoe.

So caught up in the sport was Waukewa, that for once he did not know when the canoe began to move more swiftly among the rocks. Suddenly he looked up. He caught his paddle and dipped it wildly into the rushing water.

The canoe swung sidewise, shivered, and held its own against the rushing water. Very slowly, inch by inch, it began to creep upstream toward the shore.

But suddenly there was a loud, sharp snap. The paddle parted in the boy's hands, broken just above the blade!

Waukewa gave a cry. He bent down and with the broken paddle fought the river bravely. But it was of no use. The racing river swept him on downward; the hungry falls roared in his ears.

Then the Indian boy knelt upright in the canoe. He faced the mist of the falls and folded his arms. His young face did not look afraid. He had lived like a brave. Now he would die like one.

Faster and faster raced the little bark canoe. The black rocks flew past on either side like ghosts. The roar of the terrible waters became like thunder in the boy's ears. But still Waukewa looked calmly and bravely ahead. He would face his death as a brave Indian should.

At last he began to chant the death song which he had once learned from the older braves. In a few moments all would be over. But he would come before the Great Spirit with a fearless chant upon his lips.

Suddenly a shadow fell across the canoe. Waukewa lifted his eyes and saw a great eagle circling close above him. Its legs hung down, and its spread of wings blotted out the sun. Once more the eyes of the Indian boy and the eagle met. But now it was the eagle that was master!

With a glad cry the Indian boy stood up in his canoe. The eagle circled lower still. The canoe flew on toward the waterfall's edge. The boy raised his hands and caught the legs of the eagle.

89

The next moment he looked down into the awful waters. The canoe was snatched from beneath him and thrown down the black wall of the waterfall. But the boy and the struggling eagle were floating downward through the cloud of mist.

The waterfall roared like a wild animal. The spray beat and blinded both eagle and boy. The air rushed upward as they fell. But the eagle struggled on with its load.

It fought its way out of the mist and the flying spray. Its great wings beat the air with a whistling sound. Down, down they sank, the boy and the eagle, but ever farther from the wall of water and the boiling whirlpool below.

At last, with a flutter, the eagle dropped on a sandbar below the whirlpool. The eagle and the Indian boy lay there for a minute, breathless.

Then, slowly, the eagle lifted itself. In a moment it soared away. Waukewa knelt on the sand. His shining eyes followed the great bird until, at last, it faded into the gray of the cliffs.

The Modern Hiawatha

George A. Strong

He killed the noble Mudjokivis,
With the skin he made him mittens,
Made them with the fur side inside,
Made them with the skin side outside.
He, to get the warm side inside,
Put the inside skin side outside:
He, to get the cold side outside,
Put the warm side fur side inside:
That's why he put the fur side inside,
Why he put the skin side outside,
Why he turned them inside outside.

From Worlds of People *by Matilda Bailey and Ullin W. Leavell. Reprinted by permission of American Book Company.*

Irrigation

Ann Nolan Clark

When my father
Needs water
For his thirsty fields,
He opens the ditches
To let the water run slowly,
Slowly,
Around the roots
Of all the growing things.

My father
Closes the ditches
To stop the water
When his fields
Have finished drinking.

My father
Opens the ditches
When it is his day
To irrigate his fields.

No one
Would take a day
That was not his
To irrigate.

No one
Would take too much water
When it was his day
To irrigate.

All Indians
Are taught,
When they are little,
That water is good.
It must not be wasted.

I have known this
For a long time.

Dear Diary

I'm <u>CRAZY</u> about my new school!!! It's not terrible, and I take back everything bad I ever said about it before. At first hardly anybody said anything to me, but Ms. Clayton (she's the substitute teacher) asked this girl to show me where to get crayons and other stuff. And guess what? Her name's Regina, too!!! ～ But everyone calls her Gina. Gina and I walked home together and she told me about the school building, the principal, and kids in our class. I do miss Sara, but Gina's fun.

P.s. Oh diary—wouldn't it be funny if a couple of best friends had the same name?

Dear Diary,
Today Gina, Gary and I ate lunch together. Gary is Gina's cousin. They're the same age and look a lot alike.

This school doesn't have a cafeteria like my last one did, so kids bring their own lunches and eat them inside. It's really messy !!!

Gary wants to be an artist. He wants to draw my picture.

Ps. Maybe when Mom gets her vacation we'll have Gina and Gary over for lunch. Mom can fix baked fish (yum yum) and tell them how her grandmother used to fix it.

Today is rainy,
but I feel brainy.

November 6

Dear Diary,

Our regular teacher (Mrs. Addams) came back today. She's OK, but Ms. Clayton is GREAT!!! I wish she could be my teacher all the time. Gina likes Mrs. Addams more.

Gina and Carla Laytee are good friends. Carla told Gina she thought Regina was a funny name for an Indian. Gina said anybody could be named Regina. Carla teased me about Gary. She's a creep.

creep.

P.s. I bet Sara and Gina would be friends. I think I'll write Sara.

Did you miss me Friday yesterday?

Dear Diary,

Today Mrs. Addams asked whose folks could talk to us about life when they were kids— like a show and tell for parents (ha ha). Oh, forgot to ask if any other people from my family could come. Bet creepy Carla'd faint if grandfather wore his headdress.

Gina wants Carla and me to go to the movies with her Sunday. I'd rather go skating.

I'm awfully glad Sara will spend the night here soon — maybe with Gina!

99

America, the Beautiful
Katherine Lee Bates

America! America!
God shed His grace on thee,
And crown thy good with brotherhood
From sea to shining sea.

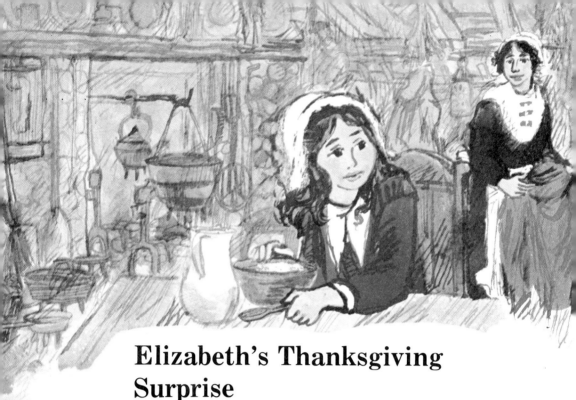

Elizabeth's Thanksgiving Surprise

"Hurry, Elizabeth," called her mother. "Your cornmeal mush will be cold."

Elizabeth jumped out of bed and quickly put on her warm clothes. She shivered in the cold morning air. She must hurry, for today there was work for everyone to do in the little colony of Plymouth. Tomorrow was the day of the big Thanksgiving feast.

Elizabeth ate her mush. As she did, she wished again that she didn't have to eat the same thing for breakfast every day. But she knew that she really should be thankful for each bite.

There had been hard years in the past. But now Elizabeth's family had plenty of food for the cold winter which lay ahead. Friendly Indians had shown the group of Pilgrims how to plant corn. And they had taught them the best ways to hunt for animals.

"At least I won't eat mush tomorrow," Elizabeth said.

"No, not tomorrow," said her mother. "Tomorrow is a special day. The men have been hunting and fishing. They have brought in wild turkey, duck, deer, fish, oysters, and clams. Tomorrow is going to be a big day of celebrating and feasting and prayer."

Elizabeth thought of the good baking odors that had filled the kitchen for days. Her mother and the other Pilgrim women had spent many hours baking and cooking. Elizabeth, too, wanted to help, but she wasn't old enough to do any of the baking. So far she had only been able to help with little jobs. If there were only something big she could do for the Thanksgiving celebration.

"I'm going to need a lot of help this morning," said her mother. "There is still much to be done. Why don't you begin by sweeping the floor?"

Elizabeth slowly picked up the twig broom and began to sweep. Her mother went to the woodshed for firewood. In a few moments she returned with a straw basket in her hands.

"Look," she said, "some animal must have helped itself to the cranberries we picked yesterday. Half of them are gone. I was just going to get them ready to cook. Now there won't be enough cranberries for tomorrow."

Elizabeth dropped her broom. She came to look at the half-empty basket. "Oh, Mother," she begged, "let me go pick some more. I know where they are. They're right along the trail, and I won't stay long."

Her mother looked at Elizabeth and then at the basket of cranberries. "I guess it will be all right, but be sure you stay on the trail. Don't wander off. Come home soon."

"I will be careful," Elizabeth promised. She took the basket and happily set off down the trail.

When she came to the cranberry patch near the path, all of the berries had been picked. There was nothing left but the vines. Elizabeth decided to go a little way into the forest to find a new cranberry patch. Soon she found one. She began to fill her basket. When the basket was almost full, Elizabeth turned to start home.

Suddenly, as though from nowhere, a large, powerful Indian appeared beside her.

"Oh!" cried Elizabeth. And grabbing her basket, she ran toward the trail. In her hurry she did not see the fallen branch that lay across her path. Her foot caught. Down she went, sprawling full length on the ground. Her basket flew out of her hands, and the precious berries scattered across the ground.

"Oh!" she cried again, this time more unhappy than surprised. Her ankle hurt, her dress was torn, her berries were gone, and towering over her was the unfamiliar figure of the big Indian. He gazed at the sprawling Elizabeth.

Gently he knelt down to help her. He almost smiled. Picking up her basket, he said, "You wait here. I bring food." Then he disappeared through the trees.

Elizabeth sat up and rubbed her ankle. She was no longer afraid. The Indian meant her no harm. She began to be very curious about what he might bring her.

She sat quietly and waited. Soon she began to wonder whether the Indian would return at all. She had almost decided to go back to the settlement when he stepped silently into the clearing. He was carrying Elizabeth's basket. He motioned toward the settlement, and she started off with the Indian helping her along.

The Pilgrims gathered around to watch as the Indian helped Elizabeth to her home. When she got to her door, he handed her the basket. Eagerly she looked to see what was in it.

The basket contained a few handfuls of corn! Elizabeth was very disappointed. Corn was not new or different. She had hoped the Indian was carrying a surprise in the basket.

She smiled at the Indian. "Thank you for the corn," she said politely, hiding her disappointment.

"This good corn," the Indian said. "You wait. You will see."

He took the basket to the open fireplace where the women had been doing much of the cooking. He greased a large pot with a strip of fat, then poured a few handfuls of corn into it. He covered the pot and set it on the hot stones of the fireplace.

The Pilgrims gathered around to watch. What a strange way to cook corn! He had not ground it, soaked it, or stewed it. He had put it dry on the fire. Surely the corn could do nothing but burn.

Soon the settlers began to hear a gentle
pop! pop! from inside the pot. The Indian
stood to one side and waited.

When the popping sounds had stopped,
he took the pot from the fire and lifted off
the lid. There was a surprised murmur
from the crowd. The pot, which had held
only a few kernels of corn, was full of fluffy
white puffs. And they smelled delicious!
The Indian smiled. Then he scooped up a
handful and held it toward Elizabeth.

"You eat," he said.

111

Elizabeth took one of the fluffy balls and tasted it. Then she took a few more pieces. They were crunchy. They were fun to eat.

And they were good! A smile crossed her face. She nodded to the others, and they all began to taste this strange new thing.

Elizabeth turned to her Indian friend. "This is very good food," she said. "Thank you very much."

Elizabeth had done something big for the Thanksgiving feast. Because of her and the friendly Indian, the Pilgrims had learned about popcorn.

Bridget Goes Prospecting

A Burro Gets a Name

Boone McBride whistled happily as he led his new burro back to camp. To have bought such a fine young animal was good luck indeed.

The next day the little burro carried a prospector's pack on her back. The pack was not heavy, and she liked being on the move. She watched her master as he chipped bits of rock while they wandered over the mountainsides.

Boone McBride was kind and gentle. The little burro trusted him. Though she did not want to go across some of the streams they came to, he never got angry with her. The days and weeks passed happily.

Adapted with permission of The Macmillan Company from Midget and Bridget *by Berta and Elmer Hader. Copyright © 1934 by Berta and Elmer Hader.*

One day the trail they were following cut across some deep wagon ruts. McBride stopped. He had not seen anyone for weeks. He knew that a farmer named O'Shea had moved here some years before.

O'Shea and his wife and two children were the only people in the valley. It had been two years since Boone had seen the O'Sheas. But he knew they would be glad to see him.

Boone turned from the trail and followed the wagon tracks. The farmhouse stood in a small clearing. A little girl about six years old stood on the porch. She stared at Boone McBride and his burro for a moment and then darted into the house.

Before Boone had come much nearer, Brian O'Shea and his wife stood in the doorway and waved. The little girl looked out from behind her mother's dress.

"Sure and it's me that said only this morning, 'Mary, it's high time Mr. Boone McBride came this way.' And here you are. And have you found that rich gold mine and—but come in, man, rest your bones. Here am I asking a lot of fool questions of you." O'Shea stopped talking. He helped take the pack off the burro.

Boone turned the burro loose in the pen behind the house. As soon as he left her, she went into the barn to see what she could find to eat.

Boone returned to the house. He knew that the O'Sheas would have a thousand questions. They lived so far away that they didn't have visitors very often. Mrs. O'Shea, fresh and pretty, seemed just a girl. It was hard for her to be living so far from other people.

The little girl, too, had a question. She asked it in her tiny voice, "What's his name?"

"That is Mr. McBride, honey," answered her mother.

"I . . . I meant the little horse's name," said the child. "What is the name of that little horse?"

"That little horse is a burro," laughed McBride. "Well . . . well, that reminds me. I have never given her a real name. Let me think. What shall I call her? I have had many burros. There was Chiquita and Pancho and Carlos and Sacramento and Bolivar." Boone counted them one by one on his fingers. "What would you name her? What is a name you like?"

The little girl hung her head. "I don't know many names. Do you think she would like Bridget? That's my name."

"It's a grand name, and I'm sure she will be proud to have it. Bridget the burro it shall be. Bring a pail of water, and we'll christen her this minute."

The child got a pail of water and went with Boone to the barn. She sprinkled a few drops of the water on the surprised little burro's nose while Boone said, "It's Bridget from now on you are. I hope you never bring disgrace on the fair name of Bridget."

They returned to the house. Bridget's brother, Danny, had come in. He was very hungry, and it was nearly time for lunch.

"Hello, Mr. McBride," he said happily. "When did you come? I didn't see you."

Bridget soon slipped outside again to see her namesake. She liked animals. But she was a little afraid of Tom and Ben, the work horses, because they were so big. Bess, the cow, was gentle as could be. But she looked very dangerous when she shook her horns or stretched her neck and mooed.

Bridget liked the burro because she was so small and looked so gentle. But as Bridget entered the barn, she heard a loud heehaw. The noise made her drop the handful of grass she had picked for the burro. She ran back to the house.

"Mr. McBride, Bridget's making awful noises," she said.

Boone smiled. "I thought I heard her calling me," he said.

Boone and the children went to the barn. The burro brayed again.

"Burros know what is good for them," said Boone. "She wants to be outdoors as long as there is any sun." He untied the halter and led the burro outside. There he turned her loose in the small field with Bess, the cow.

"Animals are like people," said Boone. "They get lonesome with no one to talk to. If I didn't have my little burro, I would get very lonesome, too. Sometimes I don't have anyone else to talk to for weeks at a time."

"Gee," said Danny. "I never knew burros could talk. Daddy always said they were stupid animals."

"Stupid!" exclaimed Boone. "Why many of those little animals are smarter than their owners. And better prospectors, too! Why, I know a burro that found a rich mine for his owner."

"Gosh, Mr. McBride! Do you think your burro will find you a mountain of gold?"

"Maybe," said Boone. "I wouldn't be at all surprised if she did."

It was with regret that the farmer and his wife said good-by to Boone the next day. They watched as he followed his little burro around the bend in the road.

Bridget Pushes On

After traveling for many weeks, Boone realized he was much farther north than he liked to be. The cool days and cold nights of late October told him it was time to be in the warm desert lands.

Slowly Bridget and Boone made their way south. Boone stopped to see his friend, Big John Carlson, a miner. Big John lived in the mountains the year round.

Big John thought Boone should stay for the winter. "Don't be crazy, man," he said. "The snow will come any day. The nearest neighbors to the south are the Moystons. We haven't heard from them in a long time, but I think they are still here. And most of the way is high in the mountains."

Boone had made up his mind to winter on the desert. Much against the wishes of his friend, he started south. He knew the trail. If snow did come, what of it? It would only be a light fall, and he would soon be out of it.

Bridget was sorry when Boone threw the pack on her back, for Carlson's burro was good company. But when she found she was headed for the desert, she hurried along the trail.

Boone made camp the third night. He thanked his lucky stars that one more day would find them at the Moyston's ranch. Bridget stayed near the campfire, eating the green grass.

Her soft nose in his face woke Boone at dawn. The little burro seemed uneasy. She felt some danger. A great quiet was in the air. Dark clouds filled the sky to the north.

The pack was on Bridget's back in a few minutes. They hit the trail. If they could get through the pass in the mountains, they would be safe. The Moystons lived in a valley at the foot of the next ridge.

Bridget and Boone pushed on. Up and up they climbed. The sky grew blacker. Sometimes it was so dark in the woods that it was hard to see the trail. Then it started to snow. The air became thicker and thicker with the falling snow.

They could no longer see the trail. But Boone had been over it many times before, and there were plenty of markers. He had marked trees and chipped signs on rocks.

They pushed on and up through the snow. Now their only chance lay straight ahead. They had to reach the pass. The snowstorm had become a bad blizzard, but there was no turning back now.

"Now we are in for it and no mistake, old girl," said Boone.

Bridget didn't like the snow blowing in her eyes and ears. But she plodded along after her master.

The wind howled about them while the snow piled up in high banks. Leading Bridget, Boone pushed on. The biting wind cut through his heavy clothes. He was cold to the bone. He felt numb. But to stop now meant certain death. He plodded along, and Bridget followed him.

They were through the pass at last. Then Boone fell. He lay quiet in the soft snow. Bridget pushed at him with her nose. Boone didn't move. Bridget bumped him harder, and Boone got to his feet. He grabbed the burro's short mane. His little pal must find the way down the mountain.

Bridget, too, was tired from the long climb, but she pushed on. Boone somehow got onto the burro's back. His head fell forward, and he put his arms around the burro's short little neck.

Bridget moved slowly and carefully on
down the trail. Sure-footed though she
was, there were times when she almost
stopped. If she stepped off the trail, she and
Boone would fall down the mountainside.

Through bank after bank of snow the
burro plodded with Boone on her back.
Bridget was tired, so very tired she felt
that she could not go much farther. Then
she saw a bit of light through the gray
snow. She knew that where a light was,
there was man, too.

At last she came to the house. She heard voices. She threw back her head and brayed. Then she waited. Why didn't they come? She moved closer to the house and brayed again.

Jerry Moyston and his wife, Jill, stopped talking. They looked at each other. Could it be that they heard the braying of a burro outside their door?

"Sounds like a burro, Jill," said Jerry. "But what would a burro be doing outside in this snow?" He opened the door and looked out.

Through the dark he saw the little gray burro standing knee-deep in the snow. And there was something that looked like a man on her back. Jerry couldn't believe his eyes.

"It's Boone McBride, Jill. He's almost frozen to death," said Jerry. "Make him a hot drink while I try and warm him up. I think he'll come out of it all right."

It was some time before Boone knew where he was. His first question was, "Where's Bridget, my burro?"

"I'll take care of her, now that you are all right," said Jerry. He put on his great coat and fur hat and went out. The burro was gone, but he followed the tracks in the snow. They led to the side of the house, where the little burro stood close to the wall. Her head and her long ears were hanging down.

"It's a medal you should get, little burro," said Jerry. "I don't know how you ever found your way here." He patted her. "Come along, I'll put you in the barn out of the wind. You rest a while, and I'll bring you a nice warm mash that will make you as good as new."

Bridget was too tired to lie down on the soft straw, but she closed her eyes. A little later Jerry came back to the barn with a pan of warm mash.

"Put that away, old girl. In the morning you won't know what a bad time you have been through." Jerry rubbed her nose gently and left the barn. Bridget ate the warm mash. Then she lay down and slept.

The next day was bright and clear. The sun shone down on the snow-covered hills. The countryside was white as far as one could see.

Boone McBride was as good as ever after a few days of rest. As for Bridget, the one night's rest was all she needed, and she was ready to start on the trail the next morning.

A week or so later, Boone thanked his friends and again took to the trail. He had enjoyed his stay with the Moystons, but he wanted to get started. He still had a long way to go.

When the heavy snows of winter had completely covered the roads and trails, Boone and Bridget were safely out of the snow country. They were slowly making their way across the sunny desert, looking for the gold that they would one day find.

OREGON OR BUST!

Off to Independence

"Pa! Pa!" shouted Jed as he darted across the barnyard. "Have you heard that the Millers are going to Oregon?"

"Yes, I know, son," said his father. "Your ma and I were talking about it just yesterday because Hal Miller has been trying to talk us into traveling with them."

"Can we go, Pa?" begged Jed. "Eb says we can get homesteading land for free and that the soil is so good it would sprout doorknobs if you planted them. And we'd have plenty to eat until we got a farm started because the streams are full of fish and the woods are full of game."

"Well, I don't know, Jed," his father said slowly. "It's not as easy as that. We've got roots here. I've lived on this farm all my life. And your ma's friends and relatives are all here. And you and Nancy can go to school here. Where would you go to school in the middle of Oregon?"

"But, Pa, we can both read. And I can teach Nancy her numbers. And you and Ma can teach us the rest."

"Well, we'll see," said Jed's father. "But I'm not making any promises."

During the rest of the week, Jed could hear his parents talking in low voices late at night. He could just barely hear a few words. "Rich land . . . a better chance for Jed and Nancy . . . farm not doing too well . . . it'll be very rough . . . a long hard trail . . ."

But the next Sunday the Millers were invited for dinner. And when dinner was over, Jed's father pushed back his chair and said, "Well, Hal, we've talked it over. Looks like we'll be going to Oregon with you and your family."

The next few months flew by. They sold the farm and most of their animals, except for their horses and two cows and some chickens. They bought a strong team of young oxen.

The huge covered wagon they bought stood in front of the house. Slowly it was filled up—a little furniture, Ma's iron stove and cooking pots, farming tools, two trunks of clothes, bedding, sacks of seed, sides of bacon and dried beef, barrels of flour, and water kegs. When they ran out of room inside the wagon, they tied things to the outside.

Finally the last day came. Ma hung the basket of chickens under the wagon. Pa brought out the team of oxen and began to hitch them up.

Just as Pa was finishing, the Miller family drove up. Hal Miller called out, "We're off to Independence! We'll meet the rest of the wagon train there in three days, and then we'll be off to Oregon, so come on!" Both drivers shouted to their oxen, and the covered wagons headed west.

At Independence they camped outside the town with all the other folks that had already arrived. Jed wanted to go into town with Eb, the Millers' oldest son, but his mother told him to stay. "We need some firewood chopped and some water brought in, Jed," she said. "After we've had our supper, everybody will have to go to bed right away. The wagon train is going to start out early in the morning, and we'll all need a good night's sleep."

Jed was out of bed the next morning before anyone else. He was so excited he could hardly stand still. "Just think," he said to himself. "There'll be deserts, and mountains—tall ones, and Indians, and mountain men, and country that nobody's ever seen before. Maybe I'll even shoot a buffalo."

Soon everyone else was up. Tents and bedding were folded up, and breakfast was eaten. Then the wagons began to move out.

WASHINGTON
Columbia River
Astoria
Fort Vancouver
Willamette River
Portland
Oregon City
IDAHO
Snake River
ROCKY
CONTINENTAL DIVIDE
MON
Fort Boise
OREGON
Fort Hall
Soda Springs
Great Salt Lake
NEVADA
SIERRA NEVADA MOUNTAINS
UTAH
CALIFORNIA
Colorado River
ARIZONA
Pacific Ocean
MEXICO
MO

CANADA

UNITED STATES

MINNESOTA

TANA

NORTH DAKOTA

SOUTH DAKOTA

Missouri River

WYOMING

WISCON

Independence Rock

Sweetwater River

Fort Laramie

Scott's Bluff
Chimney Rock

South Pass

Courthouse Rock

NEBRASKA

IOWA

ILLIN

Mississippi River

St. Joseph
Liberty

Fort Leavenworth

COLORADO

Arkansas River

KANSAS

Independence

MISSOURI

OKLAHOMA

ARKANSAS

THE OREGON TRAIL

NEW MEXICO

Red River

UNTAINS

Rio Grande

TEXAS

On the Oregon Trail

The first few weeks were easy. Endless prairie stretched on as far as the eye could see. The big oxen plodded on and on. Sometimes Jed walked beside the wagon. Sometimes it was his turn to tend the herd of cows and extra horses that followed the train. Some nights he helped watch the herd, or he went to find water for cooking and washing. But he never had to chop wood. There were no trees, so someone had to gather the buffalo chips that lay all over the prairie for the cooking fire.

As they inched toward the west, the prairie changed. The grass was thinner. There were fewer watering places. The sun beat down on the travelers and beasts.

Now everyone wanted to be at the front of the wagon train. The ground was so dry that the wagons stirred up thick clouds of dust. The wagons at the end of the train had to pass through everyone else's dust. Everyone was burned brown by the sun and caked with the fine dry powder.

One day it was Jed's family's turn to be at the front of the train. Jed was walking along beside the wagon, looking ahead at the dry prairie. Suddenly he called, "Pa, look! What's that? See, up ahead, sticking up into the sky!"

"That's Courthouse Rock," Jed's father answered. "They say that it looks just like the courthouse in St. Louis. Next to that is Jail Rock, and beyond that is Scott's Bluff. Once we've passed Scott's Bluff, it won't take us long to get to Fort Laramie. Then you'll see your first mountains. Beyond the fort are the Laramie Mountains."

A week later the wagon train rolled into Fort Laramie. The train had been on the trail for seven weeks, and everyone was glad for a rest. The oxen had grown thin and tired. Wagons needed repairing. Everyone's clothes needed washing. And it was good just to sit for a few days, instead of rolling and jolting across the endless prairie lands.

Fort Laramie was a lively place. The
Indians came to trade beaver skins for
cloth and rifles. The traders came for the
rich furs. Mountain men wearing buckskin
passed through, silent and strange.

From morning to night Jed was never
still. After he finished his chores he was
free to wander around the fort, watching
and hearing everything.

But after five days it was time to push
on. Their trail leader didn't want to be
caught in the mountains by the first snows.

Beyond Fort Laramie the trail was steep
and stony. The oxen strained against their
yokes day after day. Then after a week
they reached Independence Rock standing
strong and big against the sky.

On they went. The trail grew steeper.
Finally one day Jed's father said, "Well,
everyone, this is it. The wagon's too heavy.
The axles on the wagon will break, and the
oxen will give out if we don't lighten the
load up."

Turning to Jed, he said, "Step to, son. We'll have to leave the stove, most of the cooking pots, and the big dresser, since those are about the heaviest things. I can do without some of these metal tools, but we have to keep the heavy wooden plow."

Jed tried not to look at his mother's face as he helped to carry the big iron stove off the trail. He overheard his father say, "I'm really sorry, Kate. I'll build you a fine big fireplace when we arrive in Oregon."

Finally they reached South Pass, where the trail was almost straight downhill. But going downhill was almost harder than going uphill. Wagon wheels were tied so they wouldn't roll, and the men held the wagons back with heavy ropes. Even so, the huge wagons slid like sleds, prodding the oxen into a wild run. Two wagons overturned. One of them was left behind.

Three weeks later their wagon train reached Soda Springs. Ahead of them stretched bare, dry land. There was almost no grass for the cattle and the oxen.

The sun shone hot, day after day.
Travelers, animals, and wagons were soon
covered with the fine white dust that lay
everywhere. The train was lucky if it made
seven miles a day.

The Last Thousand Miles

The days of travel seemed like one great, hot thirst. Everyone stared ahead, red-eyed and tired, looking for signs of water. Several times the cattle had to be whipped and frightened away from the water holes they found, for often the water was poison.

Along the trail lay heaps of furniture, trunks of clothing, barrels of books, and even piles of food that the travelers before them had had to leave behind. Oxen and cattle had died along the trail, and their white bones lay in the hot sun. Jed even saw a few rough crosses beside the trail. Cattle were not all that had died.

Their own oxen were dangerously thin. And their food supplies were getting low. Jed couldn't decide if he was more hungry than thirsty or more thirsty than hungry or more tired than both.

But one evening after they made camp, Jed's father said, "Well, we don't have far to go now. By tomorrow night we should be at Fort Hall. Two rivers meet there, and we'll be able to get water and food. We'd better let the oxen and cattle rest for a few days 'cause it'll be a rough trip across the mountains."

As soon as the party left Fort Hall, they followed the winding Snake River to the Oregon border. When they started out Jed said, "Pa, it shouldn't be too bad now that we're following the river 'cause at least we won't have to worry about water."

But they *did* have to worry about water. The winding Snake River cut through a wild, narrow valley. Wagons had to travel on the high, flat land above the river. The banks were so steep that sometimes they had to lower a man and a bucket with a rope just to get drinking water.

Then the trail began to climb again. "Jed," his father said, "we're almost to the Oregon border. After the border, we turn north through the mountains until we hit the Columbia River. Then we can build flatboats and travel down the river to the Willamette Valley. That's where we'll have our farm."

"Why can't we have the farm just on the other side of the border, Pa?" asked Jed. "Why do we have to go to the Willamette Valley?"

His father smiled. "You'll see why when we cross the border," he answered.

Jed saw why. The eastern part of Oregon was some of the roughest country he had ever seen. "And I thought the Laramie Mountains were bad," he thought to himself. He was hanging on to one of the ropes that kept the wagon from sliding too fast down a slope. "Up and down, up and down. I hope I never see another mountain as long as I live."

And then there were the rivers. Jed couldn't remember how many rivers they had crossed on their trip, but it seemed like these were the worst.

For one thing, they were icy cold. Often they had to swim the cattle across the deep parts, and everyone arrived on the other side wet and cold.

Sometimes they were shallow enough to walk through, and the wagons were just driven across. But the current was usually very fast, and the bottom was rocky. Two wagons had turned over, and one ox had drowned.

Finally they reached the slopes above the Columbia River Valley. Jed stood still for a minute, looking at the rich, green, rolling land below him. His father came up behind him.

"Well, there you are, Jed," his father said. "Got any doorknobs you want to plant? It almost looks like they could grow here. From here on it's going to be easy. Down the Columbia to the Willamette, and we'll be home."

Home! Jed looked slowly around him. Two thousand miles back was a small farm they had left. But now this rich grassland, these mountains, these tall trees were home. Suddenly he could hardly wait.

He jumped into the driver's seat and shouted to the oxen. They moved slowly off toward the river.

Boasts and Brags

Out West the country was bigger ...

We've got mountains so high they have to bend over to let the moon go by.

And we've got plains so wide the sun knocks a chunk of dirt off them when it squeezes past in the morning.

...the weather was worse...

We've got some pretty hot summers around here. In fact, one summer we tried to raise popcorn. But it got so hot that all the popcorn out in the fields popped before we could do anything about it. And to make matters worse, our farm animals thought it was snow, and all of them froze to death.

The next summer it was so hot that not a
drop of rain hit the ground. It all turned
into steam. That made fog so thick that we
never even watered the animals. They just
drank the fog. It was pretty funny to see
the hogs with their noses up in the air,
rooting around for fish and frogs.

People had to go around in pairs that summer. One person held the fog apart while the other one walked through.

Our neighbor, Joe, was trying to put a roof on his house that summer. But the fog was so thick that he nailed the roof onto the fog, thirty feet above the house.

Our winters are pretty rough, too. One winter it was so cold that whenever someone spoke, the words froze in midair. We had a real noisy spring when all those words thawed out.

. . . the animals were stranger . . .

We've got some real funny wild animals around here. There's the high-hen. She lives on the mountainside and lays square eggs so's they won't roll off the mountain.

And we've got the gwinter, who lives on another mountain. He's got two long legs on the downhill side and two short legs on the uphill side. He can only run in one direction—straight forward, 'round and 'round the mountain.

They're really kinda scarce now, mostly because they fight so much. A right-long-legged gwinter will meet a left-long-legged gwinter, and they tangle. The only way the weaker one can get away is to turn right around through himself—inside-out, just like a sock.

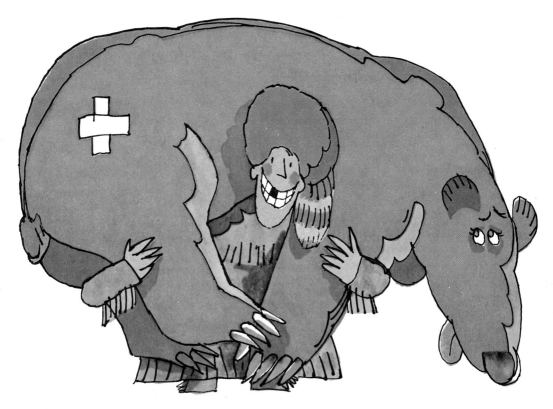

 ... and the people were toughest of all.

Now you finish this tale.

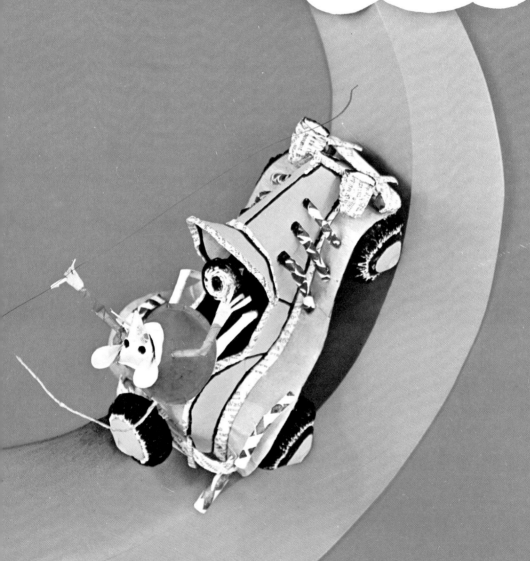

East of the
Sun, West of
the Moon

Roads Go Ever Ever On

J. R. R. Tolkien

Roads go ever ever on,
    Over rock and under tree,
By caves where never sun has shone,
    By streams that never find the sea;
Over snow by winter sown,
    And through the merry flowers
      of June,
Over grass and over stone,
    And under mountains in the moon.

From The Hobbit by J.R.R. Tolkien. Reprinted by permission of the publisher, Houghton Mifflin Company. Reprinted by permission of George Allen & Unwin Ltd., London.

The Small Yellow Train

"David," said Aunt Melissa, "there are times when I truly believe your questions will drive me crazy!"

"He's at it all day long," said Aunt Ann. "'What makes the steam engine go? How big is it? And what does it look like?' I can't answer the questions. Why do folks want to bother their heads about those new-fangled affairs, anyway?"

"Why, indeed!" agreed Aunt Melissa.

David said nothing for a few minutes. He was sorry he had annoyed the aunts. They had been so kind to him since he had come to stay with them. Maybe he should not talk so much about the new train—not even if all the town of Albany were talking about it.

"I didn't mean . . ." said David.

"Neither did I," said Aunt Melissa.

"Well," said Aunt Ann, "I've heard there is a man in town who is showing a picture of the steam engine. Perhaps if we took David to see it, he would find the answers to some of his questions."

David sat up straight, his eyes shining.

"Good," said Aunt Melissa. "We'll go this very afternoon."

So, like most of the other people in Albany, the aunts and David went to see the picture. It was cut out of black paper. It had been made by a man who had ridden on the train the first time that it carried passengers. He was showing it to people and charging a small fee for them to see it.

As David went into the room, he gasped. There was the picture. It stretched all the way across the wall from one side of the room to the other.

All the people were talking about the picture. "It's wonderful!" they said. "Just like magic. Cut out of black paper with a pair of common scissors. And look at the engineer! It's David Matthews himself. He's not quite as large as life, but twice as natural!"

It was hard to get David away from the picture of the train. He could have looked at it all day long.

"Now he'll be satisfied," said Aunt Ann.

But David was not satisfied. He had a great many more questions to ask, and he wanted to see the train with his own eyes.

At last the day came when he found courage to tell the aunts. He wanted more than anything in the world to ride on the small yellow train. When he told them, they were shocked.

"Have you heard all of the tales of what happened on that first trip?" they asked. "It jerked so that Sally Jones was thrown from her seat. Her father lost his hat and never did find it again!

"And the sparks! Mrs. Burton had a big hole burned in her new dress. The ladies who were in the open cars had to put up parasols to keep the sparks and cinders off their clothes. Sally said that her face was covered with soot.

"It is a very remarkable invention, David. But it is a most dangerous way to travel."

All of this did not discourage David. In fact, he knew he would never be quite happy until he rode on the train.

The aunts knew this, too. So, because they were really very fond of David, they began to talk together.

"He does so want to go on it," said Aunt Melissa to Aunt Ann.

"Perhaps it is not so bad after all. I hear they have made the train better," said Aunt Ann. "Sally always makes things seem worse than they are. Elizabeth does want us to visit her in Schenectady. Do you think we might try it?"

David could hardly believe his ears when the aunts told him they had decided to travel by train. When the day came, it was bright and sunny. It took quite a while to get ready.

Both aunts wore their second-best silk dresses. David's hair was brushed to a remarkable neatness.

The aunts hired a carriage to drive them to the place from which the train started. And since this was David's special day, they let him ride in front of the carriage with the coachman.

David braced his feet hard against the dashboard. He looked sideways at the coachman.

There was silence for a long time. Then the coachman looked at David and said, "Going to ride on the train, I hear."

"Yes," said David.

"H'm," said the coachman. "More time than sense. What do folks want with them steam engines anyway? They puff and snort and scare the horses half out of their wits. Thirty miles an hour it goes! I say no good will come of people shooting around the country like skyrockets. I say, give me horses!"

David could think of nothing to say. He hoped Aunt Ann and Aunt Melissa had not heard the coachman, for they might decide to turn back. Then they reached the place from which the train started.

The little engine stood on the track, puffing as if it were in a hurry to be off. It looked just like the picture. And sure enough, there was David Matthews, the engineer! The tender with wood for fuel was next to the engine. Behind that were the coaches, bright yellow with orange trimmings.

Some of the passengers wanted to sit on top of the coaches. The aunts, though, were sure it would be safer inside. Besides, they remembered about the sparks.

Now they were all seated. The conductor came to collect the tickets.

"All aboard!" The conductor climbed on a small seat behind the tender and blew a long blast on a tin horn. "All aboard!"

"Can't we get out now, before it starts?" asked Aunt Ann, opening and closing her hands with worry.

"Don't be silly, Ann," said Aunt Melissa. "We must do it for David's sake." Her voice was firm, but her knees were trembling.

S-s-s-ssss! A great sound of steam.

S-s-s-sss! Chuff! They were off!

The ride was jerky, but not nearly as bad as Sally Jones had said it was.

How quickly they traveled! The coaches rocked and swayed. The engine puffed out great clouds of black smoke.

The aunts sat stiffly, their hands folded tightly in their laps, looking very, very frightened. David looked very, very happy. He talked all the time.

"We're out in the country now! Oh, look at those cows; they're scared of us!

"Look at those children on the fence. They're so surprised to see me riding on the train!" David talked on and on.

"O-oh! We scared a horse! See him go down the road? Ouch! There's a spark on me. It's all right, I put it out.

"Your cheek is all black, Aunt Melissa. No, not that one, the other one.

"There's another horse that's scared! I wonder what he thinks we are."

After a time David did not talk so much, and the aunts didn't sit so stiffly. By now they were getting quite used to riding on the train.

Soon Aunt Ann began to look out of the window with a good deal of pleasure.

"After all, Melissa . . . " she said.

"After all, you *like* it, don't you, Aunt Ann?" asked David.

Aunt Ann looked the other way. Aunt Melissa answered.

"Why, David, it seems almost pleasant. We shall probably ride on the train a number of times."

With a deep sigh of happiness, David leaned back in his seat.

"I'll go with you every time," he said. "And when I grow up, I'll drive an engine, just like David Matthews. Won't that be fine, Aunt Melissa?"

Song of the Train

David McCord

Clickety-clack,
Wheels on the track,
This is the way
They begin the attack:
Click-ety-clack,
Click-ety-clack,
Click-ety, *clack*-ety
Click-ety
Clack.

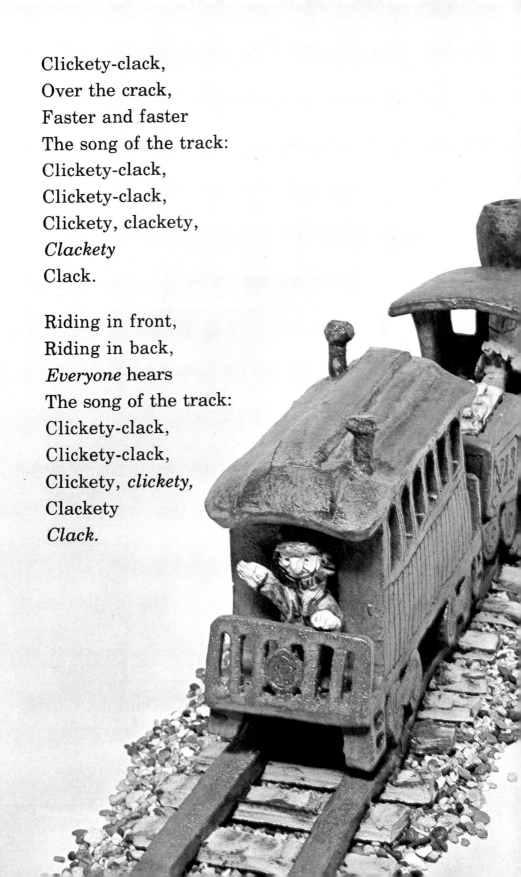

Clickety-clack,
Over the crack,
Faster and faster
The song of the track:
Clickety-clack,
Clickety-clack,
Clickety, clackety,
Clackety
Clack.

Riding in front,
Riding in back,
Everyone hears
The song of the track:
Clickety-clack,
Clickety-clack,
Clickety, *clickety,*
Clackety
Clack.

The Whimsymobile

Just look at today's highways. Car horns beep, honk, and toot. Black smoke and smelly fumes fill the air. People sit for hours in their cars just waiting for traffic to move. While they sit, all they can see are rows of cars.

The car was supposed to make things better for people. It was supposed to make travel fast and more enjoyable. But just look at the highways. What a mess!

A man named Roland Emett thought the highways were a mess, too. Mr. Emett likes to think of new things to make. So he thought of a new kind of car that would not be noisy or make the air dirty. He built the car and called it a Whimsymobile.

The Whimsymobile starts with a chug, oompa sound and runs on after-shave lotion. It has a harp instead of a loud horn.

At the back of the car is a place to cook snacks. There are also special places where pets and babies can ride.

Information courtesy of Borg-Warner Corporation and Carl Byoir & Associates, Inc.

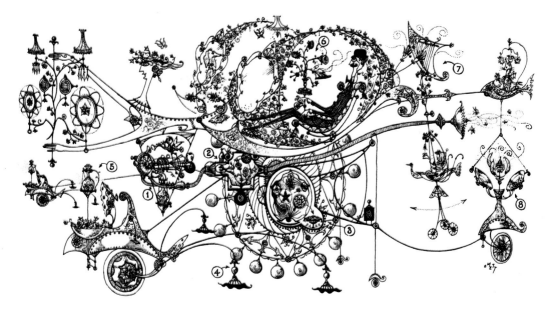

1 Power Plant
2 Anti-Pollution Unit
3 Solarmatic automatic
  Sun and Planet Transmission
4 Pussiefoot System of Hover Feet

5 Cut-glass
  fog lamps
6 Control Bouquet
7 Self-Playing Harp
8 Retractable Barbecue

Pieces of dirt in the air are gobbled up by a steel snap-dragon and then passed through sweet smelling flowers. This helps to clean and sweeten the air.

Wait, Mr. Emett! You've got to be kidding. People can't drive a car like the Whimsymobile. Why, even the name *Whimsymobile* lets us know that you've created something for fun. After all, one meaning of "whimsy" is "make-believe."

The Whimsymobile is a joke—isn't it?

Song of the Open Road

Ogden Nash

I think that I shall never see
A billboard lovely as a tree.
Indeed, unless the billboards fall
I'll never see a tree at all.

182

The Traveling Musicians

Characters

NARRATOR

DONKEY

DOG

CAT

ROOSTER

FIRST ROBBER

OTHER ROBBERS

NARRATOR: Near the town of Bremen lived a farmer and his donkey. All his life the donkey had worked hard for the farmer, but now he was old and tired. The farmer planned to put an end to him. But when the donkey saw that the farmer had such a plan, he took himself off and began to travel the road.

DONKEY: I may be worn out from plowing the farmer's pumpkin patch, but I have been told I have a fine voice, and that is worth something. I will travel to Bremen and seek my fortune as a musician.

NARRATOR: The donkey had traveled but a little way when he spied a dog lying beside the road. The dog was howling softly to himself.

DONKEY: Whatever is the matter, friend? Why are you howling so sadly?

DOG (*softly and sadly*): *ROwwwwww!* My master thinks I am too old to hunt and so he hopes to kill me tomorrow. But I have run away and hope to seek my fortune someplace, far away. But, woe is me, what am I good for? How can I make a living?

DONKEY: Oh, so that is your problem. You need not worry, for I am also seeking my fortune and am on my way to Bremen to become a traveling musician. You have a fine voice, even if it is a bit sad. Why don't you come with me, and we will see what you can do?

NARRATOR: The dog said he was willing. And so the two of them trotted along together. They had not gone far when they met a cat. She was sitting in the road and meowing to herself.

CAT: *Meowwww. Meowwww.*

DONKEY: Pray tell us, good lady, what is the matter? You don't seem to be in very good spirits.

CAT: Woe is me! How can I be in good spirits? I like to sit by the fire and drink my bowl of milk. But I'm too old to chase mice. Now my mistress won't have me. She says she will drown me in the lake, and so I have run away. But what shall I do now?

DONKEY: Oh, is that all that bothers you? Then come with us. You have a good singing voice, so you can join our band. We are going to Bremen to be traveling musicians.

CAT: *Meowwww.* Thank you kindly. I will gladly come with you.

NARRATOR: So the three of them set out— the donkey, the dog, and the cat. After they had traveled a way, they saw a big rooster standing high on a gate. He was crowing with all his might.

ROOSTER (*very loudly*): *Cock-a-doodle-doo! Cock-a-doodle-doo!*

DONKEY: What a fine song, Sir Rooster. With such a loud voice you must indeed be a happy animal.

ROOSTER: Happy? How can I be happy when tomorrow I will be cooking in my master's pot?

DONKEY: Pray tell us, why is that?

ROOSTER: Alas! My master says I sing too loudly and wake him too early. He wants to have me cooked for his Sunday dinner.

DONKEY: We three are traveling together to seek our fortune as musicians. Perhaps, with your exciting voice, you would like to join us. We all agree you'd be the hit of our band.

ROOSTER: *Cock-a-doodle-doo*! That is a fine idea! Yes, I'll come with you.

NARRATOR: And the company of four musicians set out for the town of Bremen. As night fell they found themselves wandering along a narrow path through a thick forest. They shuffled through the dark woodland until the donkey had an idea.

DONKEY: Sir Rooster, if you fly up to the top of that tree, perhaps you will be able to see the lights of Bremen.

ROOSTER: Certainly. (*He flies to the tree top.*) I cannot see the lights of Bremen, but I do see a light coming from a nearby house.

DONKEY: We had better go there. I don't wish to sleep out here in the forest.

DOG: Besides, they might have a bone or a bit of meat. I am growing hungry.

CAT: And I would like a nice fire to warm my paws.

NARRATOR: So the rooster flew back down out of the tree, and they all set off for the light. As they drew near, the light became brighter and brighter. Soon they saw a house. The donkey, being the tallest, crept up to the window and peeped in.

ROOSTER: Well, Friend Donkey, what do you see?

DONKEY: Why, I see a table, loaded down with good things to eat. And there are robbers! They're sitting around, eating and drinking.

DOG: That would be a fine place for us. But how can we get rid of the robbers?

CAT: I have a plan. Friend Dog, if you climb up on Donkey's back, then I will get on your back. Then, Rooster, if you fly up and perch on top of me, I will give a signal. When I give the signal, we will all sing in our loudest voices.

NARRATOR: So they did just that. At the cat's signal, they all sang.

DONKEY: *Heehaw! Heehaw!*

DOG: *ROwwwwwwww!*

CAT: *Meowwww! Meowwww!*

ROOSTER: *Cock-a-doodle-doo!*

} (*together*)

NARRATOR: The singing frightened the robbers so much that they ran from the house as fast as they could go.

ROBBERS: Help! Help! A terrible monster! We must hide in the woods!

NARRATOR: Now that the robbers were gone, the four friends entered the house. They sat down and ate at the big table. Then, being tired, each animal found a bed for the night.

DONKEY: I will sleep outside here on this nice bed of straw.

DOG: And I will sleep on this mat behind the door.

CAT: *Meowwww.* This fire is still warm. I will sleep on the rug beside it.

ROOSTER: And I will perch up here on the roof of the house.

NARRATOR: No sooner had the animals found their places than they fell sound asleep. The robbers had been watching from the woods. They saw the lights go out in the house.

FIRST ROBBER: Look! The lights went out. The monster must be asleep. I will go back and see if I can find a way to get rid of him.

ROBBERS: Go carefully. Don't forget his terrible cry!

NARRATOR: So the first robber crept up to the house. Finding everything quiet, he decided to light a candle. He thought the eyes of the cat were live coals, and he held the candle to them for a light.

CAT (*jumping up and very angry*): *Meow! Sppffft!*

FIRST ROBBER: Help! The monster!

NARRATOR: The cat scratched at the robber, who was pushed into the dog and bitten on the leg. The robber stumbled and fell over backwards and, while trying to get up, was kicked out the door by the donkey just as everyone was making an awful noise.

DONKEY: *Heehaw! Heehaw!*

CAT: *Meow! Sppffft!*   } (*together*)

DOG: *ROwwwwww!*

FIRST ROBBER: I've been hit with a club; someone save me from the monster!

NARRATOR: By this time the rooster had awakened, and he began to crow loudly.

ROOSTER   (*loudly*):   *Cock-a-doodle-dooooo!*

NARRATOR: The robber ran back as fast as he could to where the others waited.

191

ROBBERS: What did you find?

FIRST ROBBER: Oh! It was awful! There was a great witch by the fireplace, and she scratched me with her bony fingers. Then a man with a knife stabbed me in the leg. In the yard was a monster who beat me with a club. And on the roof sat a judge. The judge was crying, "Bring him up here! Bring him up here!"

ROBBERS: Well, we can never go there again. That much is clear. Let's get out of here before they catch us.

NARRATOR: And so the robbers fled from the country. The four friends were very happy in their new home. And it is said that they are still there today, eating and singing.

Curtain

Three Strange Creatures

Arnold Spilka

I've never seen
A Pokey doo
a Himldee
Or Snemifoo.

A Pokey doo
Has 9 big feet,
A Himldee
Has horns that meet.
And if you see
3 heads of blue
You'll know it is
A Snemifoo.

I'm told they all
  Live on the moon.
  I must go there
  . . . but
            not
                too
                    soon.

193

East of the Sun, West of the Moon

The Bear's Bargain

Long, long ago, at the edge of a sunless and gloomy forest, there lived an old man and his wife. They were very poor, and their chief pleasure lay in eight delightful children. Even though they loved all eight of their children dearly, their favorite was the youngest, Erendel.

One evening as the old couple sat and watched their children dance, the wife said, "Husband, I have been thinking. Is it not a great pity that we are so very poor? Our children are as beautiful as princes or princesses, yet they have nothing but rags to wear and rye bread to eat. If we were rich, what wonderful things we could do for them, Erendel most of all. She is the most beautiful and could marry a fine prince if we were rich."

The old man said nothing. He knew his wife was right, but there was nothing he could do about it.

One night a heavy knock sounded at the
door of their cottage. "Well, my husband,"
said the old woman, "go see who that can
be at this hour."

So the old man went outside. He stayed
so long that the old woman put her ear to
the door to listen. But all she could hear
were low voices. When her husband came
back, his face was as white as the pale
winter moon.

"What was all that?" asked the wife.

"It was a bear—a great white bear," he said, his voice shaking.

"Don't be silly," said his wife. "Do you think I'll believe anything?"

"I'm telling the truth," answered her husband. "The bear spoke to me so nicely. He said he had great powers. He said he could make us as rich as we could wish."

"Really?" said the old woman. "What did you tell him?"

"Wait," said the old man. "There's more to it. He wants one favor in return. He wants . . . he wants Erendel for his wife. He said he would make her happy . . . that she would live like a princess. I didn't know what to say to him, so I told him to come back in one week for our answer. We will have to think of something. We can't give him Erendel."

The two old people went to bed. But the wife lay awake thinking. By morning she had made up her mind.

"You know, my husband," she said, "the bear did say he would make Erendel happy. And if we don't do as he says, she will never live like a princess. And think what we could do for the other children if we were rich."

And so she argued for three days. Then finally the man threw up his hands and said, "Well, then, you take care of it. I'll have no hand in the affair. Talk to Erendel if you wish, but I hope she refuses."

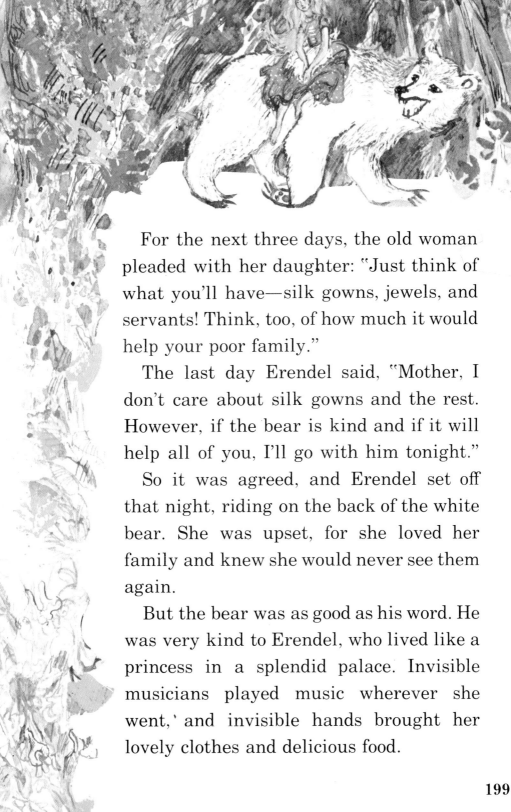

For the next three days, the old woman pleaded with her daughter: "Just think of what you'll have—silk gowns, jewels, and servants! Think, too, of how much it would help your poor family."

The last day Erendel said, "Mother, I don't care about silk gowns and the rest. However, if the bear is kind and if it will help all of you, I'll go with him tonight."

So it was agreed, and Erendel set off that night, riding on the back of the white bear. She was upset, for she loved her family and knew she would never see them again.

But the bear was as good as his word. He was very kind to Erendel, who lived like a princess in a splendid palace. Invisible musicians played music wherever she went,' and invisible hands brought her lovely clothes and delicious food.

199

But every night the shaggy white bear disappeared from the palace. As soon as it started to get dark, he would bid Erendel a good night, and she would not see him again until the sun came up the next day.

Erendel wondered about this. She had come to love the bear, and she missed him when he was gone.

Then one night, as Erendel lay awake in her bed, she heard a noise. It came from the next room. It was the bear!

Carefully, Erendel lit a candle and crept quietly into the room where she had heard the noise. There was no sound now.

Still holding the candle, she tiptoed across the room to the bed. She leaned over the bed, hardly daring to breathe.

What a surprise! The white bear was the handsomest Prince she had ever seen. She couldn't believe her eyes. She leaned closer to have a better look. Just then her hand trembled, and three drops of hot wax fell onto the prince's shirt. He woke and jumped up.

"Erendel!" he cried. "Do you know what you have done? Now there is no hope. I must leave you forever."

"No, stay here. Tell me what I have done," cried Erendel. She caught hold of his sleeve. "Why must you go?"

"It is a cruel story," said the Prince. "The Queen of Trolls has put an enchantment on me. I am a bear by day, and I am myself only after midnight. If you had been content to live with me for one year without knowing who I was, the enchantment would have been broken. We could have stayed together forever. Now I must go to the castle that lies east of the sun and west of the moon. And there I must marry the Troll Queen's daughter. Her daughter is very selfish and greedy and cruel, and she has a nose that is three yards long!"

"I will follow you," said Erendel. "I will find you wherever you are. There must be some way we can stay together. I will break the enchantment."

"Ah, Erendel," said the Prince. "You may try, but no one has ever found the castle which lies east of the sun and west of the moon. Farewell, my Erendel."

In an instant everything vanished—Prince, palace, servants—everything. Erendel found herself sitting on the grass in a dark forest.

The Impossible Journey

She wept for a long time before she dried her eyes and said to herself, "I'm being silly. If I'm to find my Prince, I must start right now," and she set off as fast as she could go.

She hastened through the forest, across green meadows, over low hills, and finally reached a high mountain. An old woman sat at the foot of the mountain, rolling a golden ball between her wrinkled hands.

"Ah, grandmother," Erendel greeted her, "can you help me to find the Troll Queen's castle? It lies east of the sun and west of the moon."

"Ah, I think I have heard tell of it," said the old woman. "But east of the sun and west of the moon—why, that's a long way off, child. I have no idea how to get to it. And why do you want to go there?"

So Erendel told the old woman the whole sad story.

"You poor dear," the old woman said. "I'll tell you what. Have a bite to eat first. Then I will lend you my horse. It will take you to my sister who lives at the foot of the Mountain of Iron. She is older than I am, and she may be able to help you. When you get there, tap the horse behind its ear, and it will come back to me. And here, take this golden ball with you. You may find some use for it."

So Erendel did as she was told. The old woman's horse galloped straight ahead, over the mountains and rivers, until it came to the Mountain of Iron. At the foot of the Mountain of Iron sat a woman older than the first. She was combing out wool with a golden comb.

"Grandmother," said Erendel. "Your younger sister sent me to you. She thought you could help me find the Troll Queen's castle. It lies east of the sun and west of the moon."

But this old woman could not help Erendel either. She told Erendel, "I have a sister who is even older than I. She lives under the Mountain of Brass. Perhaps she can help you. Take my horse. And take this golden comb. You may find a better use for it than I."

The old woman's horse galloped straight ahead, over plains and deserts, until it came to the Mountain of Brass.

But even the oldest sister didn't know the way to the castle that lay east of the sun and west of the moon. After she heard Erendel's story, she sat for a long time, spinning wool with her golden spindle.

"Well, child," she said at last. "My oldest brother is the North Wind. He travels all over the world. Perhaps in his travels he has seen this castle that lies east of the sun and west of the moon."

So Erendel and the old woman started out to find the North Wind. After a long, slow journey they arrived at the North Wind's cave. Erendel could hear a great roaring even before she saw the cave.

"What's that noise?" she asked.

"Oh, that noise is just the North Wind sleeping. You should hear him when he wakes up!" answered the woman.

When the North Wind came out of his cave, he gave a great yawn that nearly blew Erendel off her feet. She had to shout her question up at him.

"Humph!" roared the North Wind. "East of the sun and west of the moon, eh? Well, yes. I blew a leaf there once. After that I was so weak that I had to lie down for a month before I could make the trip back.

"Don't know if I can get you there, but I'll give it a try. Climb on."

So the North Wind puffed and panted
and blew himself up so huge that Erendel
was almost frightened. But before they
began their long journey, the oldest sister
tossed her golden spindle up to Erendel.
"Take this," she called. "You may find it
can help you!"

Off they went. Erendel looked over the
North Wind's shoulder. Down below, there
was a great storm. Rain and hail and snow
were falling, all at once. Trees bent to the
ground. Houses blew over.

Then they were crossing the ocean, as
under them great waves crashed and ships
sank. And still on they went.

Hours passed. The sun rose and set. On
they went through the night.

Finally Erendel could see a little light shining in the East. They were still over the ocean. But the North Wind was getting tired. Lower and lower he flew. Erendel could almost feel the salt spray. "Just a little further on! Please," she begged. "I can see land!"

With his last breath the North Wind blew Erendel onto the land. And there, just ahead of her, she could see the Troll Queen's castle. She turned to thank the North Wind, but he had gone to sleep, right there on the ground.

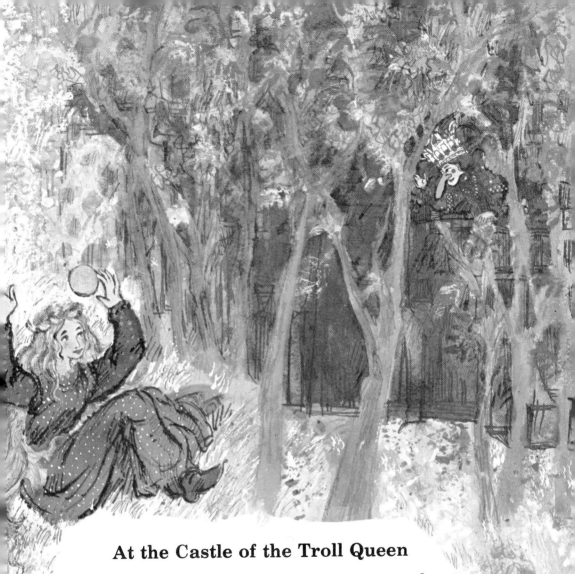

At the Castle of the Troll Queen

As Erendel hastened toward the castle, she began to prepare her scheme. "First," she thought to herself, "I must figure out a way to see the Prince alone, and I believe I can use the golden ball."

So she seated herself beneath the west windows of the castle and started to sing and to toss the golden ball.

It wasn't long before a curious face appeared at a window; then Erendel peeped up and spied the Troll Queen's daughter— the one with a nose three yards long.

"Goodness!" said the Troll Princess, "I must have that shiny golden ball. What'll you take for it?"

"It's not for sale," said Erendel. "I will not sell it for all the jewels in your castle."

"But I want it! I want it!" said the Troll Princess. "I will do anything to get it."

"I will give it to you for a favor," said Erendel.

"Anything!" said the Troll Princess.

"You may have it if I may stay one night by the Prince's bedside," said Erendel.

"That's simple," said the Troll Princess. "Now give it to me." And she took the ball.

But that evening she gave the Prince a special drink. It would make him sleep so soundly that a hundred armies could not awaken him.

The Troll Princess did not quite trust
this girl who played with a golden ball. So
when Erendel sat beside the Prince's bed,
he was sound asleep. She shook him and
called to him, but he wouldn't wake up.

The next day Erendel decided to try
again. She sat under the castle windows
where she sang and combed wool with her
golden comb.

Soon the Troll Princess stuck her head out. When she saw the comb, she wanted to buy it. Just as on the day before, Erendel asked to sit by the bed of the Prince that night. The Troll Princess agreed.

But this night was the same as the last. The Troll Princess had given the Prince the special drink, and he wouldn't wake up. Erendel shook him and called to him, then sat down by his bed and cried.

All the same, she wanted to see him just once more. The next day she sat singing and spinning with her golden spindle. The Troll Princess promised Erendel that she could sit by the Prince's bed that night, and she took the golden spindle.

Inside the castle the Prince's servants were talking to him. "Do you know," they said, "that a beautiful girl has been by your bed for the last two nights? She has shaken you and called to you, but you wouldn't wake up."

"It must be Erendel," he said to himself. "And there must be something in that drink that makes me sleep." So that night he threw the drink out the window and lay down to wait for Erendel.

When she came they laughed and cried and talked for half the night. Then the Prince stopped laughing.

"Tomorrow I am to marry the Troll Princess," he said. "But I have a plan. Remember when you dropped the wax on my nightshirt? Tomorrow I will tell the Troll Queen that I want to find out if her daughter is a good housekeeper. I will give the nightshirt to the Troll Princess and say that the one who will be my wife must be able to wash out the wax. But a troll can never wash anything clean. Then you must come in and wash the shirt clean. It is the only way we can stop the wedding."

So the next day the Prince gave the nightshirt to the ugly Troll Princess. She scrubbed and scrubbed, but the spots only got bigger and darker.

Soon her mother took the shirt, which
she scrubbed and scrubbed, but it got
dirtier and dirtier.

Then the Prince inquired, "Why not let
the girl who sits outside the castle try?"

"It can't do any harm," answered the
Troll Queen. "If we can't get out the stupid
dirt and wax, she can't either. Let the
stranger try."

Delighted to go in, Erendel entered and
took the shirt. She dipped it in the water
once; she dipped it in the water twice;
she dipped it in the water a third time,
and it came out bright and spotless.

The Troll Queen and her daughter were so furious that they turned white, then red, and finally burst.

The enchantment was broken. Erendel and the Prince returned to their palace where they lived happily ever after. And Erendel was always very kind to bears.

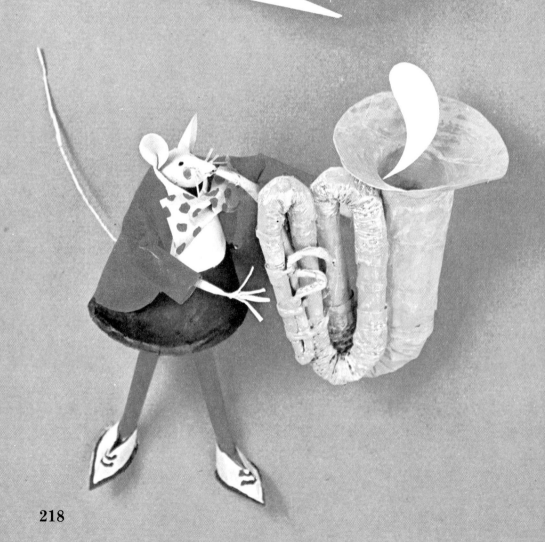

Green Grow the Rushes-O

Old Counting Song

I'll sing you one-ho,

Green grow the rushes-o!

One is one

And all alone,

And ever more shall be-o!

Numbers Old and New

Counting

" . . . 97, 98, 99, 100. Ready or not, here I come!"

Hide-and-go-seek is a simple game to play. Yet boys and girls ten thousand years ago didn't play it. They couldn't play it. They couldn't play it because they couldn't count to a hundred. They couldn't even count to three!

People then did not know much about numbers. Some groups had names for one and two but not for three and four. For all numbers that were larger than two they said "many."

This caused a lot of problems. "Many" could mean only three, or it could mean a thousand. People were never quite sure.

Shepherds were among the first people to use any kind of numbering system. They had a terrible time keeping track of all their sheep. And so a few shepherds got together and came up with a plan.

Each morning one shepherd would sit by the sheepfold. Beside him would be a big pile of pebbles. As each sheep walked from the fold into the field, the shepherd would put one pebble into a bag. After all the sheep had walked by him, the shepherd would tie up the bag of pebbles. Then he carried the bag with him as he watched the flock of sheep.

At night when the sheep walked home, the shepherd would again sit in a place where the sheep had to walk by him. As each sheep walked by, the shepherd would take a pebble out of the bag. After all the sheep were safe in the fold, the shepherd looked in his bag. If there were any pebbles left in the bag, the shepherd knew that all of the sheep were not there. He knew that for every pebble left in the bag there was one sheep missing.

But there were still some problems. If a shepherd had a very large flock of sheep, his bag of pebbles was too heavy to carry. So he learned that he could group ten of the small pebbles together and exchange them for one larger pebble. This made many less pebbles to carry.

As the years passed, people learned how to do more things. They began to grow grain and raise animals. They made many things in their workshops and began to buy and sell them. They had to know how to count and measure and figure. So they learned more and more about numbers.

Before people learned to write numbers down, they had made up names for them. Since winged animals had two wings, they used a word that meant wings for "two things." They used the name of a fruit that grows in a cluster of four to mean "four things." For "five things" they used a word that meant hand. For anything over "five things" they used a combination of the first five numbers.

About 5000 years ago, the Egyptians used pictures to show the numbers. This picture writing was the beginning of a number system which was based on 10. We still use this system. Below are symbols the Egyptians used.

The numeral for 3 looked like this:

The numeral for 12 looked like this:

The numeral for 111 looked like this:

The numeral for 1326 looked like this:

Can you write some yourself?

There is no end to the numbers we have. The numbers we use for counting go on and on. They are like the rungs of a ladder. The number one is like the first rung. And the number two is like the second rung. Counting is like climbing up the ladder. After every number there is always one more number. So this ladder has no top.

Counting in Groups

We need a name for each number in the ladder of numbers. But if we used a new word for each new number, pretty soon we would run out of words. And it would be very difficult to remember all the different number names. So people began counting in small groups. Then they could make up names for large numbers by putting together the names of small numbers.

A tribe of hunters in Australia counts things in groups of two. Their word for one is *enea*. Their word for two is *petcheval*. They do not have a special word for three. They call it *petcheval-enea,* which means two and one. For the number four they say *petcheval-petcheval,* which means two and two. Using this system, what do you think five would be?

We count things in groups, too. But we use groups of ten. We see this in the names we use for many of our numbers.

For the next number after twelve we say *thirteen.* This word is made up of two parts. The *thir* means *three,* and the *teen* means *ten.* So *thirteen* is *three and ten. Fourteen* is *four and ten.*

The word *twenty* is also made up of two parts. The *twen* means *two,* and the *ty* means *ten.* The two parts are put together to mean *two tens. Thirty* means *three tens. Forty* means *four tens,* and so on. When we say *forty-three,* we are really saying *four tens and three.*

To count a pile of pennies, first we make stacks with ten pennies in each stack. Then we count the stacks. If there are four stacks and three extra pennies, we know that the number of pennies is *four tens and three,* or *forty-three.*

Why do we count things in groups of ten? One of the reasons is that we have ten fingers. Long ago when people had to count many things, they matched them against their fingers. First they counted out enough things to match the fingers of both hands. Then they put these things aside in one group. If there were more than ten things to count, they formed more groups. We might call our numbers *two-handed numbers,* because they grew out of people counting things on two hands.

Some people had *one-handed numbers,* too. Because there are five fingers on one hand, they counted things out in groups of five. One-handed numbers were used by the people who lived in Italy over two thousand years ago.

The people who lived in Rome used the one-handed numbers. So we call their written numbers *Roman numerals.*

In Roman numerals I stands for one, and V stands for five. To write six, the Romans wrote VI, which means *five and one.*

Sometimes people counted things in groups of twelve. We still use the twelve-in-a-group system sometimes. When we count out eggs, we count out twelve at a time, and we call a group of twelve a *dozen*. When we measure things with a ruler, we count out twelve inches to make one foot. When we look at a clock, we count the hours from one to twelve and then start with one all over again.

Thousands of years ago in a country called Babylonia, the people used to count things in groups of sixty. We still use the sixty-in-a-group system when we measure time. There are sixty seconds in a minute and sixty minutes in an hour.

" . . . 97, 98, 99, 100." Simple counting. But it has taken people hundreds of years to make up the number systems we use in our daily lives.

The Count of Coursington

What the Count Wanted

The Count of Coursington had almost everything a count could wish for. He had a castle in the country. He had a cook with a secret recipe for lemon cream puffs. He owned a pair of high leather boots, a jeweled walking stick, and a cape with his name on it. He even had a wooden music box that played "Three Blind Mice."

But with all of those things the Count of Coursington was not happy. He didn't know how many cream puffs he had eaten at tea. He wasn't sure whether his music box played a tune about two, three, or ten blind mice. His problem was as simple as one, two, three—the Count of Coursington didn't know how to count!

He could recite the alphabet as quickly as he could click the heels of his boots. He knew several poems by heart. At most things he was really quite clever. But whenever he tried to think about numbers, he thought about something else instead.

He thought about elephants with ivory tusks, a tiger with stripes, or a pond full of ducks. He thought about warm gingerbread, blueberry pie, and going to sleep.

But even going to sleep was a problem. He pulled his covers up. He kicked them off. He sang himself a lullaby.

"If only I could count sheep," sighed the Count. "Oh, well. Tomorrow I will *really* think *hard* about numbers. And I *will* learn how to count."

But every tomorrow was the same. He ended up thinking about everything but numbers.

He was never quite sure what time it was. He couldn't remember if two o'clock was before seven o'clock or after five. If he had to be somewhere, he was always very late or terribly early. Sometimes he even arrived on the wrong day.

"You can't count on the Count," said the people of Coursington. "A count who can't count is sure to amount to zero."

Before long the people were so unhappy with the Count that they didn't ask him to go anywhere or do anything.

He sat all alone in his quiet country castle, eating cream puffs. Some days he sat in the kitchen, and some days he sat in the parlor. Some days he sat in his money room, surrounded by stacks and stacks of golden coins.

"What good is all this money? I cannot even pass the time by counting it," sighed the Count. "Something must be done!"

The very next day the Count put on his leather boots and his long cape and walked into town.

In the very center of town there stood a huge old tree. The Count took a piece of paper from under his cape. He hung the paper on a nail in the tree. Printed on the parchment in bright red raspberry juice was this announcement:

"Please be advised that the Count of Coursington is offering a great many golden coins to anyone who can help him solve his problem."

Sir Rocco to the Rescue

As soon as the Count had placed his notice on the tree, he made his way back to his castle. He had been home no more than a minute when there came a knocking at the Coursington castle door.

The Count opened the door. In stepped a man as round and plump as a freshly picked peach.

235

"Your worries are over," said the man. "Sir Rocco at your service. I can solve every problem. Satisfaction seven days a week."

"How nice of you to come to see me," said the Count.

"Just one thing before we begin," said Sir Rocco, seating himself comfortably in a chair. "Might I ask for just a taste of tea? So often solving problems tires one before one even begins."

"Of course," said the Count. He went to the kitchen to get the tea.

After three crumpets and two cups of tea, Sir Rocco looked around the room. "I saw your notice, printed so nicely in red raspberry juice," he said. "You wouldn't happen to have an extra little dish of ripe raspberries, would you?"

"Of course," said the Count again. He prepared a heaping plateful.

"They taste as good as they look," said Sir Rocco. "Now then, how many golden coins shall I receive as a reward for solving your problem?"

Sadly and slowly the Count shook his head. "That," he replied, "is the problem. I cannot count out coins—not the smallest amount. You see, stated quite simply, I just can't count."

Upon hearing this Sir Rocco, who had just popped another raspberry into his mouth, started laughing. Then he began to cough. "A spoonful of honey," he spluttered. "Or certainly I will choke."

Once again the Count of Coursington ran into the kitchen.

"I'm sorry I laughed," said Sir Rocco. He licked the spoon quite clean. "It's not often one meets a count who can't count. And I must admit that I was expecting a much harder task than teaching you numbers. I could teach you to stand on your head or to say *abracadabra* backwards.

"That is very kind of you," said the Count. "But I have very little need to stand on my head. I don't even say *abracadabra* frontwards. All I want to do is learn to count."

"No sooner said than done," said Sir Rocco. "However, I find I do work better on a full stomach. Perhaps a bun with butter and another bit of tea will help me work."

After Sir Rocco had eaten, he said, "Now we are ready to begin. I shall say the numbers out loud, and you repeat them to yourself."

"One, two, three," said Sir Rocco.

"Bun, chew, tea," thought the Count. He then thought about berries—raspberries, strawberries, blackberries, blueberries— but he did not think about numbers.

"Thank you for your trouble," said the Count. "But I'm afraid you have not solved my problem."

"How would you like to learn to turn a somersault?" asked Sir Rocco. He stood up, brushing the crumbs off his jacket.

Sadly the Count shook his head.

"Well, then," said Sir Rocco, "I really must be off. But do you think you might have something handy I could nibble on along the way?"

The Magic Box

It was even harder than usual for the
Count to fall asleep that night. He was still
awake when again there came a knocking
at the door.

The Count ran down the stairs and
opened the door. There stood a strange man
with a long gray beard. He was holding a
small box.

"I have in here," said the old man, "the
answer to your problem."

He held the box up so that the Count could look at it. It was made of wood, and the top was carved to look like flowers. Little colored stones formed the center of each flower. There was a lock on the box, and that, too, was shaped like a flower.

"Surely," thought the Count, "such a fine box must have something wonderful in it. In no time at all now, I will know how to count."

"Won't you come in?" asked the Count. He led the man into the parlor and watched as the box was placed very gently on the floor.

The man gave a little sigh. He looked fondly down at his box. "As old as I am," said the man, "this box is even older. It has traveled several times around the world and back again. Who knows what secrets it has held?"

"Won't you open it?" asked the Count.

The old man sighed again. Then with one hand he raised his long beard. There, hanging on a ribbon around his neck, was a key.

The Count watched as the man put the key in the lock and turned it.

In the wooden, carved, stone-encrusted, round-the-world-and-back-again box, were *peas*! But, no, they couldn't be. The Count rubbed his eyes. He scratched his head. And then he looked again. Peas! Dried, hard little peas!

"But these are peas," said the Count. "What good are peas?"

"You can hold them, you can eat them, you can roll them on the floor. You can put them in your pocket. You can keep them in a box," answered the man.

"But how can you learn to *count* with peas?" asked the Count.

The man took a pea out of the box and handed it to the Count. "Now I shall teach you how. I have given you one pea," said the man.

"Thank you," said the Count, since he did not know what else to say.

The man handed him another pea. "Now I have given you two peas," he said.

Three peas, four peas, five peas, six peas—until the Count held ten peas in the palm of his hand.

"See how simple it is?" said the man. He took the ten peas back. "We shall start again," he said. "One pea, two peas, . . ."

The Count thought about the peas—peas in a box, in a box with a key. But not once did he think about numbers.

"I'm afraid this isn't helping me," said the Count.

The man shrugged his shoulders. He took his peas and put them back into the box. He locked the box and put the key on the ribbon over his head and under his long gray beard.

"Counting counts," he said. With his box under his arm, he left the castle.

"I know that counting counts," sighed the Count, "but it seems I shall never learn how to do it."

244

In the days that followed, many people knocked at the castle door. Everyone in Coursington had heard about the Count's problem. Everyone thought he could solve the Count's problem. But none of them could help the Count count. He grew paler and more tired and more unhappy with every passing day.

"I have tried everything," said the Count sadly. "And everyone has tried to help me. The man who can solve every problem could not solve mine. A wise man with a long beard and a wonderful box that has been around the world and back again couldn't help. The people of Coursington do not have the answer for me. I shall never learn how to count. So there is just one thing left for me to do. I will forget about counting," said the Count.

The Count began to think. He tried to think about all the things he tried not to think about before.

But he could not think about elephants with ivory tusks or a tiger with stripes or a pond full of ducks. He couldn't think about raspberries, strawberries, blackberries, or blueberries. He could not think about peas in a carved box. He couldn't think about jumping rope, climbing trees, or flying kites.

No matter how hard he tried to think about polka dots and dragons, apricots and wagons, anything, everything, or something else, all he could think about were *numbers.*

"One, two, three, four, five, six, seven, eight, nine, ten," thought the Count. "One, two, three, four, five, six, seven, eight, nine, ten. One, two, three . . ."

And with a smile on his face, the Count fell fast asleep!

Girls Can, Too!

Lee Bennett Hopkins

Tony said: "Boys are better!
  They can . . .
    whack a ball,
    ride a bike with one hand
    leap off a wall."

I just listened
  and when he was through,
I laughed and said:

  "Oh, yeah! Well girls can, too!"

Then I leaped off the wall,
  and rode away
With *his* 200 baseball cards
  I won that day.

248

two friends

Nikki Giovanni

lydia and shirley have
two pierced ears and
two bare ones
five pigtails
two pairs of sneakers
two berets
two smiles
one necklace
one bracelet
lots of stripes and
one good friendship

Jamila

Morning sunshine danced through the blinds covering Jamila Clay's bedroom window. Jamila, lying on her bed, was talking to her new pet.

Pets had not been allowed in the building where the Clays had lived before, but still Jamila had always wanted a pet. When the Clays moved to a new apartment, Jamila got a little green turtle and named it Sue. Nobody would laugh at a plain name like Sue as they always did at the name Jamila.

Jamila could still recall that terrible day last year in her old school when Tom Johnson had hooted, "Hey, look at old Meeba-Deeba who use to count money for the Queen of Sheba! Your mother must have been stuck with a pin just as she was thinking of a name for you. And *Jamila* is what she shouted." All of the children on the playground roared with laughter as Jamila lunged toward Tom Johnson.

"You take that back, you big bully," she shouted. Jamila knocked Tom's pointing finger away from her face and glared at him.

"Meeba-Deeba is mad, kids!" Tom shouted as he pushed her. Jamila pushed and hit Tom back. Then a fight started. It was always like that for Jamila when the kids learned her name. She wished she could keep her name a secret.

Jamila never told her parents about the fights and how she felt about her name. They were both so proud of *Jamila*. Mrs. Clay couldn't remember where she had heard the name, but she loved the way it sounded. She thought it was a name anyone would be proud to have.

"You'd better hurry, Jamila," Mrs. Clay called from downstairs. "You don't want to be late on your first day in the new school, do you?"

Jamila turned over on the bed and looked at the clock. It wouldn't take long to walk the two blocks to school. But she hated to face the crowd of laughing children she knew she was going to meet.

Jamila put Sue into her dress pocket and started off for school. She walked slowly so she wouldn't get to school until the last bell rang. By then all of the children would be in the building, and no one could ask what her name was until she got to her room. Then the teacher wouldn't let them laugh at her.

As Jamila walked bravely into the class-room and over to the teacher's desk, two children singled her out and started to giggle together. Jamila was especially puzzled when others started to laugh at her before she even mentioned her name.

"Look at that head!" shouted one boy as another hooted with delight. By now, everyone was laughing and shouting as they pointed to Jamila. Then she glanced down at her skirt and discovered her turtle's head peeking out of her pocket!

"Why don't you put your turtle on the desk so your classmates can come up and see it," suggested Ms. Williamson, smiling.

Jamila put the turtle on the desk. The children gathered around it. "What's your turtle's name?" asked Ms. Williamson.

Jamila quickly said, "Jamila." She waited for the laughter of the children to start. But there was no laughter.

Ms. Williamson said excitedly, "Oh, that's a good name! And this turtle certainly is a good-looking one. Is that why you picked an African name that means *beautiful*?"

"What?" asked Jamila. She stood puzzled, looking at Ms. Williamson. "I don't understand what you mean."

"The name Jamila means *beautiful* in Swahili." said Ms. Williamson.

"Jamila is a name often given in East Africa to the child who is thought to be the most beautiful in a family," said Ms. Williamson. As she talked, she picked up the turtle and placed it in a bowl of water with rocks on the bottom.

"Now, children, go back to your seats," said Ms. Williamson, "and give our new classmate a chance to tell us her name."

Ms. Williamson looked at Jamila, and Jamila told the class her name. Then she explained why she had said that Jamila was the turtle's name. Again she waited for the laughter to start.

"Ms. Williamson, how did you know that Jamila was an African name?" asked a tall girl.

"I wonder what my name means," said a boy with lots of black hair.

"How can I find out what my name means?" asked another boy.

"All right, everyone," said Ms. Williamson. "Here's a book that tells what names mean and where they come from. We can look in it later today. But it's important to remember that not all names are listed in this book. We can look for other books that tell about names, too."

Jamila smiled as she walked to the desk that Ms. Williamson had picked out for her. "I already know what my name means," she thought. "And until today I never understood what a beautiful name it really is!"

Metric Names and Numbers

When is it colder?

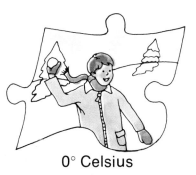

32° Fahrenheit   0° Celsius

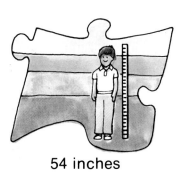

Who is taller?

54 inches   about 141 centimeters

Which weighs more?

about 20 pounds of spaghetti   9 kilograms of spaghetti

For the answers, turn the page upside down.

In each puzzle both parts are equal.

⚑ What's in a Name?

A family named *Zylch* changed their name to *Aaaba*. When they were asked why they chose another unusual name instead of a simpler one, they said, "We don't mind having an unusual name, but we want one that will come first in the telephone book."

What would you call yourself if you were going to change your name? You might pick the name of your favorite TV star or sports hero. Perhaps you could invent a name that no one else has but you. You might choose a name just because you like the way it sounds or because you like what the name means.

Many names have a meaning. *John,* for example, is a Hebrew name that means "God is gracious." *John* is such a popular name that it appears in some form in many languages. In French, *John* is *Jean,* and in Italian, it is *Giovanni.* In Spanish, *John* is *Juan;* in Scottish, it is *Ian;* and in Russian, it is *Ivan.*

In some instances the meaning of a child's name tells something about the child and about the traditions of the family. In Japan, the first son in a family might be called *Taro,* which refers only to the firstborn son. The Ashanti tribes in Africa sometimes name children for days of the week. A baby born on Thursday could be called *Yaw,* because the Ashanti word for Thursday is *Yawada.*

259

American Indians sometimes give names that will describe a person. An Indian boy might be named *Thunder Cloud* because he always seems to be frowning. An Indian girl might be called *Running Brook* because she always seems to be free, happy, and full of life.

Many times names are chosen to honor a relative or to carry on the name of a family, but parents don't always know the meaning of the name they choose.

Many parents like to choose a name that makes people think of courage, beauty, or history. But some names are picked because people think the names are clever. Girls have been named *June Bug, Penny Bank,* and *Polly Parrot.*

Boys have been called *Donald Duck, Billy Goat,* and *Peter Rabbit.* A music teacher in Paris named seven of his children for each note of the scale. They were called *Doh, Ray, Me, Fah, Sol, La,* and *Ti.* His eighth child was named *Octave!*

All over the world, babies have been named for colors, flowers, animals, days of the week, months of the year, jewels, saints, and stars. The Kwakiutl Indians in North America give a child one name for the winter and another for the summer.

A girl from Liverpool, England, had one of the world's longest names. Her parents, to honor all letters of the alphabet, named her *Anna Bertha Cecilia Diana Emily Fanny Gertrude Hypathia Inez Jane Kate Louise Maud Nora Ophilia Quince Rebecca Starkey Teresa Ulysis Venus Winifred Xenophone Yetty Zeno!* (Have you noticed which letter is missing? Her last name was *Pepper!*)

Luckily, the little girl from Liverpool didn't always have to say her whole name. She was simply called *Annie.*

Names are fun to think about. Have you thought about yours?

Days and Weeks and Centuries

The Name of the Day

Have you ever been curious about how the days of the week were named? It happened thousands of years ago.

During ancient times people thought there were seven planets, including the sun and the moon. Each different planet, they believed, controlled a different hour of the day. Each day was named after the planet that supposedly ruled the first hour of that day. This belief explains how Sunday (the sun's day) and Monday (the moon's day) got their names.

The ancient people worshiped gods they identified with the planets. These pages show the planets and the names they share with the gods. Although most of the names we use to label the days are Norse, many countries use the Roman.

From About the History of the Calendar *by A.E. Evenson, published by Childrens Press, Chicago.*

DAY	NORSE	ROMAN
Sunday	Sun	Sol
Monday	Moon	Luna
Tuesday	Tiw	Mars
Wednesday	Woden	Mercury
Thursday	Thor	Jupiter
Friday	Frigg	Venus
Saturday		Saturn

The Day of the Week

You probably know the date, the month, and the year of your birth, but do you know what day of the week it was? You can discover it for yourself by using the unusual calendar on pages 266 and 267. It is called a *perpetual calendar,* and it includes every year in the twentieth century. This is how simply it works.

Imagine that your birthday is August 15, 1970. Under the year column put your finger just below 70. Now move your finger straight across the page to the August column. You should be pointing to the letter *G*.

Look at the calendar marked *G* and locate the number 15. It is under Saturday. So, if your birthday is August 15, 1970, then you were born on a Saturday.

These calendars show thirty-one days in the month. But some months have only thirty days. This will help you remember:

> Thirty days have September,
>> April,
>>> June,
>>>> and November.
>
> All the rest have thirty-one,
>> Except—
>>> you know which one.

Now use the perpetual calendar to find the day of the week on which your birthday fell. Then check back to discover what planet the ancient people thought ruled your day. You might look up the birthdays of your friends and family, too.

A Twentieth Century Calendar

Year				Jan.	Feb.	Mar.	Apr.	May	Jun.	Jul.	Aug.	Sep.	Oct.	Nov.	Dec.
1901	29	57	85	C	F	F	B	D	G	B	E	A	C	F	A
02	30	58	86	D	G	G	C	E	A	C	F	B	D	G	B
03	31	59	87	E	A	A	D	F	B	D	G	C	E	A	C
04	32	60	88	F	B	C	F	A	D	F	B	E	G	C	E
05	33	61	89	A	D	D	G	B	E	G	C	F	A	D	F
06	34	62	90	B	E	E	A	C	F	A	D	G	B	E	G
07	35	63	91	C	F	F	B	D	G	B	E	A	C	F	A
08	36	64	92	D	G	A	D	F	B	D	G	C	E	A	C
09	37	65	93	F	B	B	E	G	C	E	A	D	F	B	D
10	38	66	94	G	C	C	F	A	D	F	B	E	G	C	E
11	39	67	95	A	D	D	G	B	E	G	C	F	A	D	F
12	40	68	96	B	E	F	B	D	G	B	E	A	C	F	A
13	41	69	97	D	G	G	C	E	A	C	F	B	D	G	B
14	42	70	98	E	A	A	D	F	B	D	G	C	E	A	C
15	43	71	99	F	B	B	E	G	C	E	A	D	F	B	D
16	44	72	2000	G	C	D	G	B	E	G	C	F	A	D	F
17	45	73		B	E	E	A	C	F	A	D	G	B	E	G
18	46	74		C	F	F	B	D	G	B	E	A	C	F	A
19	47	75		D	G	G	C	E	A	C	F	B	D	G	B
20	48	76		E	A	B	E	G	C	E	A	D	F	B	D
21	49	77		G	C	C	F	A	D	F	B	E	G	C	E
22	50	78		A	D	D	G	B	E	G	C	F	A	D	F
23	51	79		B	E	E	A	C	F	A	D	G	B	E	G
24	52	80		C	F	G	C	E	A	C	F	B	D	G	B
25	53	81		E	A	A	D	F	B	D	G	C	E	A	C
26	54	82		F	B	B	E	G	C	E	A	D	F	B	D
27	55	83		G	C	C	F	A	D	F	B	E	G	C	E
28	56	84		A	D	E	A	C	F	A	D	G	B	E	G

A

Sun.	Mon.	Tue.	Wed.	Thu.	Fri.	Sat.
1	2	3	4	5	6	7
8	9	10	11	12	13	14
15	16	17	18	19	20	21
22	23	24	25	26	27	28
29	30	31				

B

Sun.	Mon.	Tue.	Wed.	Thu.	Fri.	Sat.
	1	2	3	4	5	6
7	8	9	10	11	12	13
14	15	16	17	18	19	20
21	22	23	24	25	26	27
28	29	30	31			

C

Sun.	Mon.	Tue.	Wed.	Thu.	Fri.	Sat.
		1	2	3	4	5
6	7	8	9	10	11	12
13	14	15	16	17	18	19
20	21	22	23	24	25	26
27	28	29	30	31		

D

Sun.	Mon.	Tue.	Wed.	Thu.	Fri.	Sat.
			1	2	3	4
5	6	7	8	9	10	11
12	13	14	15	16	17	18
19	20	21	22	23	24	25
26	27	28	29	30	31	

E

Sun.	Mon.	Tue.	Wed.	Thu.	Fri.	Sat.
				1	2	3
4	5	6	7	8	9	10
11	12	13	14	15	16	17
18	19	20	21	22	23	24
25	26	27	28	29	30	31

F

Sun.	Mon.	Tue.	Wed.	Thu.	Fri.	Sat.
					1	2
3	4	5	6	7	8	9
10	11	12	13	14	15	16
17	18	19	20	21	22	23
24	25	26	27	28	29	30
31						

G

Sun.	Mon.	Tue.	Wed.	Thu.	Fri.	Sat.
						1
2	3	4	5	6	7	8
9	10	11	12	13	14	15
16	17	18	19	20	21	22
23	24	25	26	27	28	29
30	31					

⌐ Fun and Nonsense

Do you like riddles? What about the ones below?

Try to answer the riddles below. If you give up, turn the book upside down.

1. What will a green pebble become if you throw it into the Red Sea?

2. What should you do if you find a fire-breathing monster at your door?

3. What is a baby elephant after he is four days old?

3. Five days old.

2. Hope that it's Halloween.

1. Wet.

268

Know any good jokes?

Can you tell any good jokes?

What nonsense is this?

shortstop

windowpane

starfish

baby bottle

mountaineers

pigpen

friendships

reading lamp

What nonsense can you make of *flower
bed, butterfly, spyglass, quarterback?*

Motor Cars

Rowena Bennett

From a city window, 'way up high,
I like to watch the cars go by.
They look like burnished beetles, black,
That leave a little muddy track
Behind them as they slowly crawl.

Sometimes they do not move at all
But huddle close with hum and drone
As though they feared to be alone.
They grope their way through fog and night
With the golden feelers of their light.

Reprinted from Songs from Around a Toadstool Table. Copyright © 1967 by Rowena Bennett, and used by permission of Follett Publishing Company.

The Life and Death of a House

The ancient building directly across the street from my house is being demolished. I've been watching the wrecking crew work.

My grandmother told me that during her childhood, the building was the big mansion of a wealthy family. The husband and wife lived there with their two children and over twenty servants.

Their mansion was surrounded by very beautiful gardens. Most evenings guests dressed in expensive silks and laces arrived in horse-drawn carriages. Then the house was filled with laughing, dancing people.

After the deaths of the wealthy couple, the children sadly moved away. The big mansion was sold and converted into a boarding house. On the spot where the beautiful gardens used to be, apartment houses were built. The house began to look a little bit shabby.

After a number of years, city inspectors came to look at the house. They told the owner he could not keep a boarding house there anymore. Now the neighborhood was only for apartment houses.

So the old house was turned into an apartment house. New walls were built where doors used to be. Kitchens were put where guests and servants once slept. Large rooms were turned into several small rooms. Thirty families moved in where one family had once lived.

Many years passed. My grandmother grew old, and the building grew old, too. The building became very shabby. Only poor people lived there. They did not have the money to rent a better place. Many things broke in the building, but the landlord didn't fix them. "It would cost more money than the building is worth," he said.

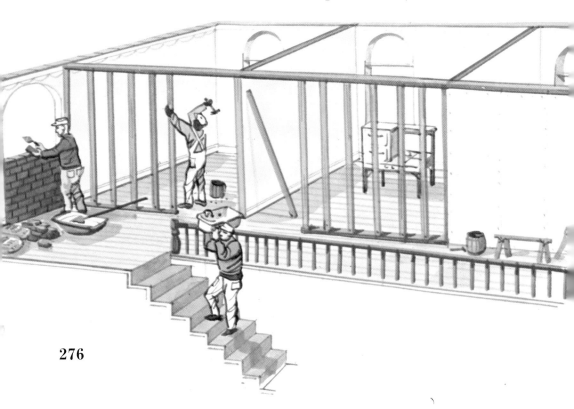

As the building grew older, the city became more and more crowded. Buildings were built higher and higher, and land became more and more valuable. At last the land on which the old building stood was worth much more money than the building. So the landlord sold the building.

The new owner didn't really want the building. He wanted the land it stood on. On the land he could build a tall new building—a skyscraper. In the same space where thirty families had lived in the old building, three hundred could live in the new one.

So the new owner told all the people in the building to move out. He gave them a month to find new places to live. Then the old building stood empty, waiting for the wrecking crew.

Today is the day of the wrecking. A few people are standing in front of the shabby old building. Grandmother and I are watching from the window of my room.

An oversized flat truck rumbles slowly down the street. On its broad back is a huge monster of a machine known as a crane. Though it is folded up, its long boom juts far out behind the truck. A red flag dangles from the boom's end, warning autos to give the truck room.

The truck pulls up onto the once splendid lawn of the building. From the back of the truck, a double ramp is lowered, and the crane is driven down.

The operator of the crane is sitting in a cab under the boom. He works the controls, raising the boom to its full height. It towers over the building.

Something that looks like the mouth of a dinosaur is hanging from the top of the boom. My grandmother tells me that it is called a *clam bucket*.

While the crane driver sets up the crane, other men drive up in cars and in trucks. They wear shiny helmets and look ready for work. Grandmother says the helmets protect the men from the falling pieces of the building.

One of the men gives orders, and the crane begins its work.

The crane driver works his controls, moving the crane closer to the building. He turns his cab until the top of the boom is right over the building.

Then, *blam!*—the clam bucket falls on the roof. *Blam! Blam!* Again and again, until the roof is broken to bits. All the bits of roof have fallen to the floor below.

The man at the controls carefully moves the crane until the clam bucket is right over the outside wall. The mouth of the clam bucket opens. It is lowered, slowly this time. Now it bites into the top of the outside wall. *Crunch!* Its jaws are full of brick and glass.

The crane driver turns the crane until
the clam bucket is right over a big truck.
Crash! The mouth opens and drops its load
into the truck.

Again and again the clam bucket bites
the top of the outside wall, dropping each
bite into the truck.

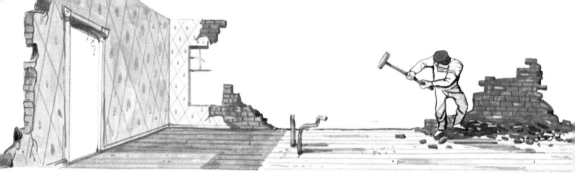

Completely filled, the truck pulls away to dump its load into a nearby landfill. Soon it will return for more of the ancient building. Meanwhile, an almost identical truck rumbles into its place.

Through the huge, crumbling holes in the top of the outer walls, we can see the faded wallpaper on the walls of the rooms inside. The doors in these walls now open into space. The sun shines briefly where it has never shone before.

The clam bucket sweeps down on these inside walls, swiftly biting them away. Soon they too are nothing but a pile of dirt and rubble in the back of the truck.

Now the clam bucket rips into the ceiling of the next story. *Blam! Blam!* The ceiling is no more. Again the clam bucket begins to bite. Everything—outside walls, windows, inside walls, broken bits of ceiling—is picked up in its great jaws. It is all dumped into the waiting trucks.

In four or five hours the house is gone. Only its foundation is left. The clam bucket goes to work on that, too. *Blam! Blam!* It pounds down, and the concrete foundation is broken into bits. These bits, too, are driven away in a truck.

Only a hole in the ground is left. Dump trucks bring loads of dirt and fill up the hole. A bulldozer smooths out the dirt until it is flat.

Now there is only a vacant lot. The old house, where so many people have lived, is nothing but a memory.

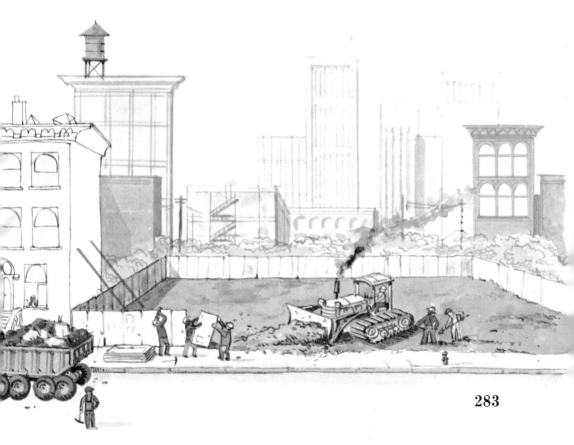

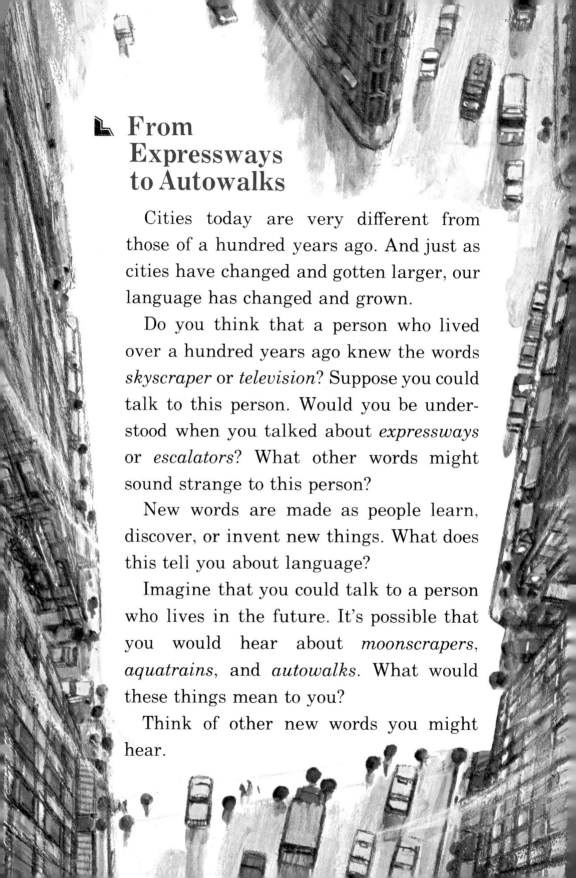

From Expressways to Autowalks

Cities today are very different from those of a hundred years ago. And just as cities have changed and gotten larger, our language has changed and grown.

Do you think that a person who lived over a hundred years ago knew the words *skyscraper* or *television*? Suppose you could talk to this person. Would you be understood when you talked about *expressways* or *escalators*? What other words might sound strange to this person?

New words are made as people learn, discover, or invent new things. What does this tell you about language?

Imagine that you could talk to a person who lives in the future. It's possible that you would hear about *moonscrapers*, *aquatrains*, and *autowalks*. What would these things mean to you?

Think of other new words you might hear.

Sunflowers for Tina

Tina wanted to grow something. The backyard had a square of dirt that might have been a garden. Nothing grew because no one had planted anything. Behind the square of dirt was a board fence that had once been painted green, and behind that was an alley.

Overhead, the laundry flapped, and sometimes a cat walked the fence, and sometimes Tina's mother leaned out of a window to talk to a neighbor in another window.

From Sunflowers for Tina *by Anne Norris Baldwin. Copyright © 1970 by Anne Norris Baldwin. Used by permission of Four Winds Press, a division of Scholastic Magazine, Inc.*

Sometimes her brother Eddie drummed on the lid of the garbage can till Tina was ready to scream, and sometimes he didn't because the lid got too hot in summer. Then he and the other boys would turn on the fire hydrant and splash quickly through the cold torrent to cool off.

Tina asked her mother if they could have a garden.

Her mother said, "No. Where'd we have a garden? A garden's a luxury. We're not rich, you know."

"Out back," said Tina, "we could have a garden. There's dirt."

"You just try and grow something in New York City dirt," said Tina's mother.

A block away, Mr. Samuels had his newsstand. He sold magazines and candy too, and sometimes he had a few bunches of flowers stuck in a pail of water.

Tina asked Mr. Samuels where he got his flowers.

"From a florist," he said.

"Where do flowers grow?" Tina asked.

"I don't know. In the country some-where. In a greenhouse, maybe."

"Don't any grow in New York?"

"I don't think so. I can't think where they would."

Tina had a dime in a handkerchief.

"What will a dime buy?"

"Lifesavers or gum."

Tina bought cherry lifesavers. When she stuck her tongue out, she could see the lifesaver on it.

The house sounded very quiet when Tina got home. Her mother was out at work. The upstairs kids weren't there. Eddie wasn't even in the backroom. Tina's grandmother sat in her corner of the bedroom, but she never made any noise. She was like a charred old stump, dark and gnarled and bent forever in the same position. Tina wished that she would only say something sometimes. Then Tina would be sure that her grandmother was really alive.

It was going to be a hot day. The kitchen smelled musty; the laundry outside hung limply; nothing moved.

Tina looked in the refrigerator. She drank a cool glass of milk and put the carton back. It was then that she noticed the bunch of bulging carrots, with tops as fresh and ruffled as Tina's Sunday dress. Lush and beautiful gardens sprang into her mind. Acres of greenery grew before her very eyes.

Very quickly, Tina untwisted the wire that held the carrots together. She took out half the bunch and carefully replaced the others. As she closed the refrigerator, the hot air from outside rushed against her face.

Tina took the carrots and a dirty spoon from the sink and went outside. She knelt down on the cracked concrete in front of the little square of earth by the fence, not even noticing that she scraped her knee. The ground was dry and hard. Tina dug at it with the spoon, but she couldn't make much of a hole. The handle of the spoon bent, and she hurt her hand trying to straighten it.

Tina went inside for some water. The faucet wouldn't stop dripping after she had filled a glass. She gave up and let it drip. She poured the water into the ground where she had been digging and went back for more. The water made digging a little easier.

At last, Tina had planted four carrots in a neat row by the fence. The green feathery tops stuck up cheerfully in the sun. She watered them lovingly.

Tina rinsed the dirt off the spoon and left it in the sink where she had found it. She heard her grandmother moving clumsily in the bedroom and went in.

"Would you like a drink of water?" she asked her grandmother. It was all she could think of. She thought of telling her about the garden, but it didn't seem worthwhile: her grandmother never answered her.

The old lady nodded silently, and Tina brought her a glass. Tina sat down on the floor at her feet. She dug the lifesavers out of her dress pocket and peeled one off for her grandmother, whose wrinkled hand shook a little as she took it.

Tina left the room and waited impatiently for her mother to come home. From time to time, she went out back and looked at her garden. The day dragged slowly on. The carrot tops began to droop in the hot sun.

From the next yard came the sound of Eddie practicing a tune on his harmonica. Tina hoped that he wouldn't see her garden before their mother did. She was sure Eddie would laugh.

Finally, the gate clicked, and Tina began sweeping the kitchen so that her mother wouldn't see her excitement. Tina's mother came heavily through the back door and began putting away a bag of groceries. Then she washed her hot face at the sink and changed into her slippers. "Phew," she said, wringing her hands. "Summer's here."

Tina danced in a circle around her broom. She did a low curtsy to her mother for fun.

"What's with you, child?"

"Oh, nothing. Didn't you notice any-thing?"

Tina's mother looked all around the room. Then she looked at Tina with a puzzled expression. Tina laughed.

"Give up?"

"Give up."

"My garden!"

Tina swished past her mother and out the door before her mother had time to be surprised. She planted herself proudly in front of the little row of drooping carrot tops and she spread out her arms happily toward the sun.

Tina's mother stood squarely in the door-way, her hands on her hips. She stared at Tina.

"What on earth . . . ?"

"I planted it myself," said Tina.

"You didn't . . . !"

"Carrots," explained Tina. "They should grow." But her voice sounded uncertain by the end of the sentence.

"Oh no," said Tina's mother with a look of dismay. "Not our supper. You just dig those right up again!"

The days passed, and the summer went right on being hot and heavy. Even the pigeons looked hot. They waddled around the flat rooftops.

Eddie got a shoeshine kit from his uncle and spent most of his time hanging around downtown where business was better.

"Why don't you find something to do?" Eddie asked Tina. "Anything's better than just sitting around."

"Like what?"

"I don't know. Help Mom."

"I do."

"You don't."

When Tina started to cry, Eddie felt sorry and said, "Well, don't feel bad. Shinin' shoes ain't no fun either."

"I wish we had a garden," Tina said. She hadn't meant to tell Eddie, but it just came out.

"A garden?" Eddie said. "What for?"

"Just to look at. It'd be pretty."

Eddie looked thoughtful. Then he said, "I'll be back," and swung through the rickety gate. She could hear him whistling as he loped down the alley.

Later, he came back and said, "I'll show you a garden, Sis," and he jerked his head toward the street.

Tina followed him some three blocks. She felt warmly happy.

Eddie stopped at the edge of an empty lot. "There," he said. "Sunflowers!"

Once there had been a building instead of the empty lot, and people had lived in it. Now nothing was left except some broken bricks.

Out of the rubble of brick and old cement, two stalks, taller than Tina herself, rose toward the sky. Each one lifted a yellow sun to light the day.

"How beautiful," said Tina. The harsh ruins of the broken building made the stalks seem remarkable. It didn't matter that they weren't her own; they were there for anyone to see.

Eddie started forward to pick them for her.

"No, don't," Tina said.

He hesitated, trying for a moment to understand the expression on her face. Then he shrugged.

Tina was thinking of something quite different. She had suddenly remembered her old grandmother, hunched and silent in her dark corner, with only the whites of her eyes seeming to move. Her life was dark and old and crumbled, like the empty lot. Tina could only guess what it once had been. There didn't seem to be any sunflowers, any bright spots at all, left in her grandmother's life.

At home, Tina put on her yellow dress. It was almost too small for her, but the color was bright and beautiful against her dark skin.

Around the bedroom she danced, and as she twirled, her full skirt filled with air and stood out from her waist, a golden disk of petals.

Tina could sense her grandmother's eyes follow her around the room questioningly.

"I'm a sunflower," Tina said.

Even though the room was very dark, Tina could see her grandmother's whole face crinkle into a smile. The whites of her eyes shone, and her thin shoulders shook under her shawl. Out of the cave between her cheeks came a distant rumble of laughter which Tina had never heard before.

The Park

James S. Tippett

I'm glad that I
   Live near a park
For in the winter
   After dark
The park lights shine
   As bright and still
As dandelions
   On a hill.

298

Manuel's Secret

Manuel lived on a beautiful island called Puerto Rico. He loved his island—a land where sugar cane grows taller than a man, where the days are always warm, and where a little tree toad called a *coquí* hums children to sleep every night.

Manuel lived with his Mamita and his Papito, his two brothers, Luís and Ramón, and his little sister, Maya. They all lived together in a little house Papito had built for them.

Reprinted with permission of Nancy Howe de Pagan.

Papito was a sugar cane cutter. Early every morning he put on his old blue shirt and his white straw hat and walked down the long road to the sugar cane fields. All day he worked in the hot sun, cutting sugar cane with a big sharp knife called a *machete.*

In the evening Manuel and his brothers, Luís and Ramón, and their little sister, Maya, would be waiting for their Papito as he walked back along the road to their home. Sometimes, far off in the distance, they could see him coming with a white package under his arm. And they knew that he was bringing them some sweet cane to suck.

In July, after all the sugar cane had been cut, Papito and the other men of the village would try to find other jobs until December when the new sugar cane would be ready to cut. The lucky ones would work in the fields clearing off the old sugar cane stalks so the new cane could be planted. But only a few men were needed to do this work, and so most of them just waited.

For the last two years Papito had been one of the ones to wait, but this year he could wait no longer. Manuel needed new shoes for school and Maya's dress was full of holes. Papito's brother, Uncle Mario, lived in New York. He worked in a factory. "Maybe there will be a job for me there," thought Papito.

So that evening Papito wrote to his brother, and he and Mamita talked late into the night.

In the morning he woke the children and told them what he and Mamita had talked about. "I cannot wait for the sugar cane harvest this year," he told them. "We must leave our island and go to New York. I will work hard. Maybe things will be better for us there."

Everyone was very excited—everyone except Manuel. He did not want to leave his beautiful island and the little wooden house his father had built.

But Luís, Ramón, and Maya were not sad. They were thinking of all the things their cousins had told them about New York. Of buildings that reach to the sky— only the mountains in Puerto Rico are that high! Trains that run under the ground— the only trains in Puerto Rico are the little puffing ones that carry sugar cane to the mill. Something strange in winter, cold and white—it never snows in Puerto Rico!

Mamita was excited, too. Her brothers and sisters lived in New York, and she had not seen them in many years. Everyone was happy, except Manuel.

"Why do you look so sad?" Maya asked her brother.

Manuel looked down at his shoes. He didn't really want a new pair. But then he looked at Maya's dress all full of holes, and he remembered how hard his father had to work, and how upset he was when he couldn't find work.

"I was just thinking," he said finally. And together they went with Luís and Ramón to help their Mamita get ready to go to New York.

"There is not much room on a plane," Mamita said, "so we must take only what we really need." Maya helped Mamita pack the suitcases with clothes. They would need warmer ones when winter came to New York. Then Mamita wrapped the two big metal bowls she used to cook rice and beans. In the afternoon, all the children helped Papito catch the chickens and take them to market to be sold. Luís and Ramón took Borínquen, the goat, to the farm of Don Tomás where he would eat grass all day and grow old and fat.

Papito would not need his machete anymore, so he let Manuel give it to his friend Arturo, who would soon be old enough to help his father cut sugar cane. Slowly, they moved everything out of the little house into suitcases or boxes, or to be sold at the market or given to friends. By evening the rooms were almost empty. Papito looked at the little house he had built. Then he looked at his children with a sad smile and said, "And now, each of you may choose one thing—something small and very special you want to take with you to New York."

Maya ran to get her doll. "I must take Una; she would be lonely without me." Luís found the whistle he had carved from a papaya branch, and Ramón took the kite he had made of bakery-bread paper.

But Manuel just stood still. Everyone waited for him to find something. "What will you take? What will you take to New York?" they asked. But Manuel did not answer. He just looked out the window, at the very beautiful valley and, beyond it, the sea. How could he choose something? Just one thing? When what he wanted most of all was to take everything—the little house, the smell of mangoes, the warmth of the afternoon sun, the sound of coquís at night.

He walked out the door to the old mango tree that stood behind the house. He climbed from branch to branch until he reached a place high above the little house. He could see the road his father walked every morning, and in the distance the green fields of new sugar cane.

Manuel had climbed the tree often; sometimes after school to suck the cane until his mother called him for supper; sometimes when he was sad and wanted to be alone. Today he was sad. "What will I take to New York?" he thought. "It must be something that will always remind me of my beautiful island!

"I could catch a little coquí to sing sweet tunes to me at night. But New York gets so cold. A coquí would not be happy there. I could pick a bright orange mango, but I would eat it on the plane, and then what would be left? Maybe I could find a big seashell to listen to the sound of the ocean, but what good is the sound if there is no warm water to splash in?"

Night was coming and the sun had almost disappeared behind the mountains. Manuel climbed down from the tree and started walking along the road to the cane fields. The coquís had begun to hum, and the night breezes carried the sweetness of sugar cane. As he walked he remembered a little song his grandmother had once taught him when he was very young. The song reminded him of the beautiful sea, of coquís and mangoes and the little house his father had built.

Maya woke him early the next morning.
"Have you found something to bring to
New York?" she whispered.

"Yes," said Manuel.

"What is it?" she cried. "Do you want to
put it in my suitcase?"

"No," Manuel smiled. "I cannot show you
now. You must wait. It is a secret. You will
see when we get to New York."

That afternoon Manuel and his family flew to New York in a big plane. Weeks passed, and they began to get used to their new life. Every morning, Papito went to work with his brother Mario.

He did not walk as he had done in Puerto Rico; he took a train that ran under the ground. There were no more days working in the afternoon sun; now he worked in a factory with big machines. The children started school with their cousins.

It was getting colder. Soon winter would come. Maya thought how warm it must be in Puerto Rico. Ramón wished he had a mango to eat. Luís missed the song of the coquí. All he could hear was the noisy sound of cars and trucks.

And then Manuel smiled. "Now you will see what I have brought with me from Puerto Rico." And he began to sing the little song his grandmother had taught him long ago. And slowly, everyone began to sing the song, over and over, late into the night—the song of coquís and mangoes and the warm blue sea of their beautiful island called Puerto Rico.

Islands of warm and beautiful seas
Warm sun and cool night breeze
Moonlight shines through mango trees
Hum me to sleep, little coquís . . . .

My Dictionary

acre: 4,840 square yards of land. *She owns ten acres of land.*

advise: to tell or inform. *We were advised that the road was closed.*

amount: to be worth. *That little bean plant won't amount to much.*

annoy: to upset, to make a little angry. *Alice annoyed her mother by being late for dinner.*

axle: a bar on which a wheel turns. *Car wheels turn on strong axles.*

beast: an animal. *We gave the beasts in the barn food and water.*

blizzard: very strong cold winds and a lot of snow. *We did not go out in the blizzard.*

bluff: a high cliff. *The house was on a bluff overlooking the river.*

blush: to get red in the face. *Jack blushed when he won the prize.*

bulge: to stick out. *Her pockets bulged with apples and cookies.*

burro: a small donkey. *A burro carried the woman's food and sleeping bag.*

butcher: to kill animals for food. *Cows and pigs are butchered for meat.*

century: a hundred years. *My house is a century old.*

charred: burned and blackened by fire. *After the fire we threw out the charred table.*

cinder: a small piece of partly burned wood that is no longer flaming. *The fire was out and only the cinders were left.*

content: happy, satisfied. *I am content to stay home when it rains.*

convert: to change from one thing to another. *The house was converted into a store.*

cottage: a small house. *Last summer we stayed in a cottage on the lake.*

current: the moving of water in a river. *The current made the boat float along quickly.*

curtsy: a bow made by bending the knees and lowering the body. *The princess gave a curtsy in front of the queen.*

demolish: to tear down, to destroy. *My little sister demolished my sand castle.*

distribute: to hand out. *Free candy was distributed to everyone.*

florist: a person who sells flowers. *We bought the roses from a florist.*

foundation: the bottom part of a building that helps hold it up. *The foundation of our house is made of stone.*

furious: very angry. *He was furious about the spilled paint.*

gloomy: dark, full of shadows. *The house was gloomy with the lights out.*

gracious: kind. *The doctor was a gracious, friendly person.*

halter: a rope that ties around an animal's head and is used for leading it. *The horse did not like to wear a halter.*

helmet: a strong covering that protects the head. *Football players wear helmets.*

hesitate: to wait a little. *The boy hesitated before jumping into the water.*

identical: the very same. *The twins wore identical jackets.*

infant: baby. *The infant cried before he went to sleep.*

inquire: to ask. *We inquired when the movie would start.*

locate: to find. *John can't locate his shoes.*

luxury: something nice that is not necessary and is often expensive. *A big car is a luxury.*

mansion: a very large, grand house. *Those rich people live in a mansion.*

nasty: mean. *The nasty pirate took the gold.*

numb: having lost the power to feel. *My fingers were so cold they were numb.*

oyster: a shellfish used for food. *We ate oysters for lunch.*

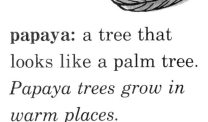

papaya: a tree that looks like a palm tree. *Papaya trees grow in warm places.*

perch: to sit on a high place. *The bird perched on the top branch.*

plead: to beg, to ask again and again. *He pleaded with his brother to come home.*

plod: to walk in a tired, slow way. *The old horse plodded down the street.*

prospector: a person who looks for gold or silver or oil. *The prospector found gold in the river.*

rapids: a place in a river where the water rushes very fast. *It is dangerous to row a boat over the rapids.*

regret: a feeling of sadness. *I felt regret at leaving my dog behind.*

remarkable: special, not usual. *The picture he painted was remarkable.*

rumble: to move with a heavy rolling sound. *The old car rumbles.*

runt: an animal or person that is smaller than usual. *When the pigs were born, one was a runt.*

rut: a long deep mark made in the ground by wheels. *The bike path has ruts in it.*

scheme: a plan. *He has a scheme to make money.*

shabby: worn out, old. *Pete's coat looks shabby.*

sopping: very wet. *After walking in the rain, my clothes were sopping.*

splendid: great, grand, wonderful. *The king wore splendid robes made of gold and silver.*

stump: the lower part of a tree left after it has been cut down. *After the trees were cut, the field was full of stumps.*

torrent: a fast stream of water. *A torrent of water rushed into the bathtub.*

untimely: too early or too soon. *We had an untimely lunch at ten in the morning.*

vacant: empty. *The family moved, so the house was vacant.*

valuable: worth a lot. *Grandfather has a very valuable gold ring.*

vanish: to disappear. *The magician waved his hand and the rabbit vanished.*

yoke: a wooden frame used to fasten two animals together. *The yoke was put on the oxen before they started to pull the wagon.*

Pronunciation Guide

	Pronunciation Respelling	Dictionary Respelling
Aaaba	(AH buh)	(ä′bə)
Apache	(uh PACH ee)	(ə păch′ē)
Apahoqui	(ah pah HOH kee)	(ä pä hō′kē)
Arturo	(ahr TOOR oh)	(är tür′ō)
Ashanti	(ah SHAHN tee)	(ä shän′tē)
Bolivar	(BOH lee vahr)	(bō′lē vär′)
Borinquen	(bohr EEN kayn)	(bôr ēn′kān)
Carlos	(KAHR lohs)	(kär′lōs)
Cheyennes	(shy EHNS)	(shī ĕns′)
Chiquita	(chuh KEE tah)	(chə kē′tä)
coquí	(koh KEE)	(kō kē′)
Don Tomás	(DAHN toh MAHS)	(dŏn tō mäs′)
enea	(EH nee uh)	(ĕ′nē ə)
Erendel	(EH rehn dehl)	(ĕ′rĕn dĕl)
Giovanni	(gee oh VAH nee)	(gē ō vä′nē)
Grupatupsky	(gruhp uh TUHP skee)	(grŭp′ ə tŭp′skē)
gwinter	(GWIHN tur)	(gwĭn′tėr)
Himldee	(HIHM uhl DEE)	(hĭm′əl dē′)
Hypathia	(hy PAY shih uh)	(hī pā′shĭ ə)
Ian	(EE uhn)	(ē′ən)
Ivan	(EE vahn)	(ē′vän)
Jamila	(jah MEE lah)	(jä mē′lä)
Juan	(hoo AHN)	(hü än′)
Kwakiutl	(kwah kee YOO tl)	(kwä kē yü′tl)
Luís	(loo EES)	(lü ēs′)

 Pronunciation Respelling system from The World Book Encyclopedia. © *1978 World Book-Childcraft International, Inc.*

machete	(muh SHEH tee)	(mə shĕ′tē)
Mamita	(mah MEE tah)	(mä mē′tä)
Manuel	(mahn WEHL)	(män wĕl′)
Maya	(MAH jah)	(mä′jä)
Mudjokivis	(muhj uh KEE vihs)	(mŭj ə kē′vĭs)
Pancho	(PAHN choh)	(pän′chō)
Papito	(pah PEE toh)	(pä pē′tō)
petcheval	(PEHTCH eh vahl)	(pĕtch′ĕ väl)
Ramón	(rah MOHN)	(rä mōn′)
Rocco	(RAH koh)	(rä′kō)
Sheba	(SHEE buh)	(shē′bə)
Snemifoo	(SNEHM ee FOO)	(snĕm′ē fü′)
Swahili	(swah HEE lee)	(swä hē′lē)
Taro	(TAH roh)	(tä′ rō)
Una	(OO nah)	(ü′nä)
Waukewa	(wah KEE wuh)	(wä kē′wə)
Xenophone	(ZEHN oh fohn)	(zĕn′ō fōn)
Yaw	(YOW)	(you)
Yawada	(YOW ah dah)	(you′ä dä)
Zylch	(ZIHLCH)	(zĭlch)

Illustrators and Photographers

Franz Altschuler   *77-91*

Bill and Judy Anderson   *277, 285-288, 290, 291, 293, 295-297*

Ted Carr   *157-163, 182, 250, 252-254, 256*

Gil Cohen   *113-116, 118-132*

Roland Emett   *181*

Winnie Fitch   *22-30*

Larry Frederick   *99*

Mae Gerhard   *31-33, 102-112, 194-217*

Morton Goldsholl Design Associates   *34-38*

George Hamblin   *193*

Jim Higa   *8, 9, 60, 100, 165, 218-225, 227-230, 272, 273*

F. & M. Higgins   *298*

Janet LaSalle   *299-311*

Dora Leder   *51-59*

Gloria Maliarek   *178, 179*

Dick Martin   *263-265*

Tom Miller   *62-76*

Phoebe Moore   *166-177*

Herb Mott   *93-96*

Howard Mueller   *10, 12-17, 19-21, 92, 133-156*

Joe Phelan   *274-276, 278-283*

Jo Polseno   *39-43, 45-47, 49, 50*

Parviz Sadighian   *257, 312-317*

Ralph Schlegel   *231-240, 242-247*

Ted Schroeder   *183-192*

George Suyeoka   *258-262*

Jerry Warshaw   *180, 268-271*

Mary Lou Wise   *248, 249*

34986